INSPIRING
TINY
HOMES

INSPIRING TINY HOMES

CREATIVE LIVING ON LAND, ON THE WATER, AND ON WHEELS

GILL HERIZ

with photography by **Nicolette Hallett**

CICO BOOKS
LONDON NEW YORK

This book is dedicated to everyone with the vision to create tiny homes for whatever reason, anywhere in the world.

Published in 2018 by CICO Books
An imprint of Ryland Peters & Small Ltd
20–21 Jockey's Fields   341 E 116th St
London WC1R 4BW   New York, NY 10029

www.rylandpeters.com

10 9 8 7 6 5 4 3 2 1

A CIP catalog record for this book is available from
the Library of Congress and the British Library.

ISBN: 978 1 78249 357 0

Printed in China

Editor: Caroline West
Designer: Vicky Rankin
Photographer: Nicolette Hallett (except images on
pp. 44–49, 68 (top left, center right, bottom left, bottom
right); 76–81, 86–89, 90–93, 120 (bottom left), and
146–147, by James Gardiner)

Art director: Sally Powell
Production manager: Gordana Simakovic
Publishing manager: Penny Craig
Publisher: Cindy Richards

CONTENTS

Introduction 6

Chapter one
Contemporary Spaces 10

Chapter two
On the Water 36

Chapter three
On Wheels 68

Chapter four
Eco Homes 120

Chapter five
Cottages and Houses 164

Index 190

Acknowledgments 192

INTRODUCTION

"Small is Beautiful"—E.F. Schumacher

This is a book about those who choose to live in different types of small-scale accommodation. The homeowners tell their personal stories, explaining how they came to "live tiny." They describe the builds and reveal what living in this way means to them. It is intended to inform and inspire the reader, and, perhaps, encourage people to think about how they live and if tiny living is for them.

Tiny homes appear to be "the new thing," either a lifestyle choice or a "glam" notion, although this is not the case for many. A lack of affordable housing and new ethics underpin the choices some people are making in order to home themselves.

When you talk about tiny homes, many people imagine structures built on flat-bed trailers, which have been springing up all over the USA and Australia, and are becoming more popular in other countries, including the UK. Although true, this is not the whole story. Indeed, people have been "living small" for centuries, and in every place, for reasons of practicality, mobility, flexibility, and choice. Also, most people in the world do not have the luxury of "living it large." Living it large only used to be for princes and barons. Now it is the aspiration of many, so they can show off their achievements and wealth by living (or not) in the largest house they can find. For many others, their choices are made because of different value systems in which small living makes so much more sense.

So, what is a tiny home? Although there is some debate about what square footage constitutes "tiny," tiny homes are basically creative solutions to ways of living; are relatively cheap to build or convert; and give their owners choices, reflecting how they want to live and impact on the world. Tiny houses are both downsizes and upsizes. They can be stunningly beautiful and imaginative. They ask that their owners be discerning regarding what belongings they have, forcing them to decide what is a necessity and what is merely beautiful. These choices are personal and can be seen as part of a movement away from money and property-slavery to a more simple and connected way of living.

There are a myriad ways of living smaller, including houseboats, horseboxes, sheds, shacks, yurts and teepees, in caravans in back gardens and fields, and in micro studios in cities. Some houses in towns and cities were always tiny and many housed whole families. New-living solutions are borne out of necessity and from choice. They are legal, "a-legal," and illegal. Some tiny-home people hide away until they feel confident about going through the official channels to become legal. This differs from country to country and from state to state, and even within cities and zones.

Tiny homes have become the answer for many people needing somewhere to live, who also possess the creativity and energy to create something different. Many tiny-home people build their own properties; they often have strong environmental credentials and want to make as little impact on the world as possible. They share a desire for simplicity and wish to get away from the world of "stuff" and consumerism. Being off-grid is the ultimate in independence from the outside world and many people in tiny homes have achieved part or all of that ambition. A smaller footprint is more environmentally friendly. One woman was even perplexed when asked to show a utility bill!

For some older people, living tiny means giving up debt and mortgages, simplifying their lives, and, best of all, feeling free to experience the life they want. Having new perspectives can give us the lifestyle we desire and open our minds to new ways of being.

Moving from a larger home to a tiny house is the ultimate lesson in de-cluttering. Over our lives we acquire, are given, and buy lots and lots of things. The William Morris quote most often used is: "Have nothing in your house that you do not know to be useful, or believe to be beautiful." Some items are useful and beautiful—most, probably, are not. If your new home is only 200 square feet (18.5 square meters) and maybe not more than 12ft (3.5m) high, what do you really, really need when it comes right down to it and what will make your new home beautiful, practical, and comfortable to live in?

Tiny-home dwellers are masters of the art of multifunctional furniture and ergonomics, with stairs doubling up as storage, shoe drawers, pull-out tables, and even somewhere to put the kitty litter! Boat people and those who have been to sea understand this art well. Every inch matters.

Tiny-home living is also becoming more popular in response to the state of the housing market in the West, which has become perverse, with most young people no longer expecting to buy a typical home and many finding it harder to keep going with debt and high rents. Indeed, massive property prices in cities have meant that even the tiniest spaces can be beyond most people's reach. In London, it is calculated that 50,000 new houses need to be built each year to meet housing demand, but even those that are

being built are never going to be truly affordable for thousands of people. Homelessness is also a huge and increasing issue everywhere, with those in power either unable or unwilling to address the causes or social and health outcomes.

Nevertheless, there is creativity in the city, too. City dwelling may include the tiniest of locations, such as garages and the gaps between buildings, being rediscovered as potential living spaces. People also build on top of existing buildings or go underground. These innovative spaces can still be very expensive, however. Micro-housing with shared facilities offers one solution. These are built in cities, much along the lines of co-housing, where people have a private space with communal facilities, so saving on space and creating a sense of community. Housing for homeless people is being created in container houses, such as those in Ealing, London, which are regarded as temporary homes that are a step toward addressing the needs of residents, and in tiny house villages, such as the one in Seattle on pages 16–21. Some feel that these initiatives are a drop in the ocean when addressing the numbers of homeless people, but they are significant and important to those who live there.

In the meantime, when conventional housing is not available, some still manage to live in cities, such as Bristol, in the UK, in vans, either out of choice or necessity. These nomads are not always welcome, but they have their own communities of like-minded people who value the low-cost freedom they have achieved. They often have jobs, work in creative ways, or are volunteers in local communities. Prejudice and fear from locals can be hard to live with, but theirs is one solution to living in an expensive city. Houseboats, too, have traditionally been a way of living in cities, but slightly apart from mainstream properties. Yet even some of these are now being bought, done up, and sold for big bucks. Nevertheless, people still live a simpler life tucked away on the water.

Quite often, it is not the build or conversion of a tiny home that is difficult, but rather finding a spot to live. Zoning and Planning Laws may restrict what can be built where, how people can live, and for how long each year. Neighbors need to be open-minded and accepting, or tiny homers can find themselves being moved on. Legality can be a gray area because the law has not really caught up with this creative way of living, with part of that creativity perhaps being how you describe your home—this might be a "studio" or "annexe," but not seen as an RV (recreational vehicle) or a separate home—and issues such as getting insurance can be tricky.

The book is divided into five chapters, covering different tiny-home categories: homes in contemporary spaces; homes on or by the water; tiny homes on wheels; eco-homes; and cottages and houses. It must be said that there is some overlap between these categories, as tiny homes on wheels may also be eco-friendly or contemporary in style or build.

Each chapter is filled with stories of wonderful tiny homes, explaining how they came about, the inspiration behind them, how practical problems were solved, and how they were built and decorated. The stories also explore what these little homes mean to those who live in them. The book includes those who live full-time and year round in their tiny homes, while recognizing that, for some, climate and other factors limit tiny-home living to a part of the year only. The people featured vary from those with the simplest and most minimal property to those for whom "tiny" is only a relative concept after downsizing from somewhere much larger. Whatever their personal circumstances, however, all the people in the book are innovative, open-minded, and resourceful, and share a love of living in tiny spaces.

Chapter one
CONTEMPORARY SPACES

The cost of land, a lack of space, and the need for affordable housing mean there are opportunities in cities for imaginative design solutions for tiny living. We see wonderful, architect-designed homes slotted into the smallest of spaces and marvel at the super-contemporary results. Most of these homes have been built on expensive land, with a high-input design and build. There are other contemporary solutions, such as the micro studios in Seattle that provide individual living spaces with communal facilities. The Tiny House Village, also in Seattle, may not be contemporary in design, but is a modern solution for some of the city's many homeless people. Similar approaches are being tried in other cities around the world, including the use of containers and prefab units to provide homes for those unable to access "normal" housing.

People are also looking for opportunities in unusual places. Linda and Antje, for example, built their tiny modern home on top of and behind an old carpenter's workshop. Loraine also turned an old workshop into a small but spacious home, while keeping the bones of the building's history. It all comes down to imagination.

Graham is all about minimalism and design, and created a light, airy forest home on an old caravan chassis in the north of Scotland, ensuring that the design and storage features would make this clever abode work for him. Clearly, contemporary design can happen anywhere—in the middle of a city or in the far north of Scotland.

There are tiny contemporary homes in other chapters, too—what they all have in common is innovative design and a clever use of materials.

LEFT The communal roof terrace is a great space for parties and social gatherings, with fabulous views over the Seattle skyscape to the sea.

OPPOSITE Above the internal courtyard, with its tables and benches, kitchen, and barbecue, is an opening to the sky, with a slab of yellow contrasting against the gray of the corrugated walls.

Micro studios are a solution to the need for low-cost homes, especially for young people living in cities. Jennifer's micro studio in Seattle has a discreet entrance on one side next to a large yellow wall. **Carly** stays there to look after the place and also Jennifer's large dog when she is away—which is often. This suits Carly down to the ground.

The "Karma" building is constructed to high ecological standards and designed to be user-friendly. Although the residents have mini-kitchen areas in their units, in the inner courtyard there is a communal dining area with a kitchen, an outside broiler (grill), and, along a corridor, a bike storage room and laundry. This means that much of the space we expect everyone to have for mod-cons, such as a washing machines etc., is provided in communal areas, as is the case in the co-housing movement, which values privacy but also offers community and the option of shared spaces and facilities.

Carly says, "It's the perfect space to expand into—especially with Apollo, Jennifer's large dog!"

Looking up when we arrive, we see a rectangle of blue sky above the bright yellow wall. Stairs to the top of the building reveal an open area with tables and chairs, as well as fantastic views over Seattle, the Space Needle, the sea, and the distant mountains. Carly says there are often get-togethers up there. On the walls of the stairwells and corridors there are "Banksy"-style murals, adding to the funkiness of the block.

The micro studio is comprised of two rooms with an entrance area. In the entrance, there are simple, white block shelves for storing all sorts of items and, on top, sits Jennifer's collection of perfume bottles. Even in this small space, not all the shelves are full. Opposite the entrance is

LEFT Every inch of space in the kitchen area is used to hang utensils and store crockery above a small, but useful, countertop. On one of the shelves is a powder-blue microwave. It matches Jennifer's much-loved powder-blue refrigerator, which is housed beneath the countertop.

the shower room, which is a good size because it was originally designed for a disabled person.

There is a double bed and also an enormous dog bed by a large window that looks out onto 12th Avenue. Opposite the bed, there's a long arrangement that includes a kitchen unit, a desk area, and clothes storage. Jennifer loves her 1950s powder-blue Daewoo refrigerator and has purchased a matching microwave. A mini-sink and the microwave provide cooking facilities if Carly or Jennifer don't want to use the communal kitchen.

There has been much discussion around micro studios in Seattle, with the question of accommodation size being one of the most contentious issues. Indeed, in March 2017, David Neuman of the Sightline Institute said, "In 2014, Seattle amended its land-use code, effectively banning congregate micro-housing (small private rooms with shared kitchens), while promoting small efficiency dwelling units (SEDUs), which are scaled-down studio apartments with complete kitchens and baths, and a minimum size of 220 square feet. As time went on, the building department (SDCI) began to tinker with the interpretation of these rules, excluding certain areas of the unit from counting toward its minimum size. The practical effect was that the

220 square feet minimum became almost impossible to achieve in real life; the smallest units expanded until they were at least 250 square feet and averaged around 280 square feet."

There were arguments about human dignity. A building regulations committee in Seattle said that "a 220 square-foot apartment is too small... it must accommodate conventional furnishings, including a bed, table, and chairs." This ignored communal cooking and eating areas and also the designs put forward by David Neuman to demonstrate workable layouts. Other issues around fire safety ignored the fact that all new apartments had building regulation fire-rated walls, floors, and ceilings, fire alarms, and sprinklers. Public health also brought up issues of psychological stress and the spread of disease, ignoring the benefits of community living, which include mutual support, shared areas, and cheaper rents. And so it went on, with supporters of micro-living spaces, with additional shared spaces, saying that the call for larger self-contained units was more about developers and profits than the needs of residents.

This resistance to reduced-space living accommodation is not only commercial and situated in an outdated planning and zoning paradigm, but precludes exciting, creative, and workable solutions for providing affordable housing initiatives for the future. Projects such as the "Karma" building and co-housing, with their emphasis on shared utilities, spaces, and communities, are often regarded with suspicion.

The "Karma" residential units clearly do not conform to the new rules, so the design and build presumably happened before 2014. These micro studios in the city, which are accessible for work, university, and a vibrant social life, do exist. Carly expresses her sense of place. She says the area is a nice neighborhood, with a "hip and young crowd. There are bars and a park nearby and it is a gay-friendly place to be." It is inexpensive with a "downtown feel."

In contrast to the critics' view, Carly says, "There is a super-friendly community feel."

BELOW There is a long wall with shelving, storage, and a small kitchen. Beyond the large dog bed is a view of the tree-lined road beneath.

After being homeless, **Bob** now lives in one of the houses in a Tiny House Village in Seattle, developed by the Low Income Housing Institute (LIHI) on land owned by the Lutheran Church of the Good Shepherd. Homelessness in Seattle is a huge issue, as it is in many cities around the world, and without shelter, people become ill and can even die.

A voluntary organization in Seattle lobbying government for the expansion of emergency shelters and for changes in Federal Law to allow self-managed encampments on public land took part in the One Night Count in January 2017, which showed that 3,000 vulnerable men, women, and children were living unsheltered on the streets of Seattle.

Tiny house villages are regarded as a means of enabling the homeless community by some people, but others see them as an excuse not to do better for thousands of homeless people in US cities. When you begin to examine homelessness, and how tiny house villages are tackling it, you encounter the world of politics and the personal stories of those given a chance to settle and find ways of moving on with their lives.

A lack of land, property prices, and exorbitant rents prevent people coming up with their own permanent solutions.

LEFT Built on land owned by the next-door church, this Tiny House Village has two rows of very tiny houses that are big enough for a bed and shelves. They provide a safe space for homeless people to live and move off the streets.

Issues of ownership, both real and motivational, are problematic. Are the people "in the community" or are they a transient, unsettled group? How much do the authorities really attempt to address the local and wider issues of homelessness? There are many questions to be answered.

There is no doubt that giving homeless people a roof over their heads and a safe place to be has helped many of them find support for their problems. This has led to the development of these "villages." Based in the village, children can go to school and health issues can also be addressed on a more regular basis. The residents can lock their doors and keep themselves and their belongings safe.

As LIHI in Seattle, explains: "A tiny house may seem like a teeny idea, but it can help save a life."

BELOW The communal showers and rest rooms in the village are a recent addition, built in timber with an attractive diagonal, tongue-and-groove fascia and a balustrade balcony.

How is it possible for tiny houses and tiny house villages to be built, given Seattle's laws on land use and its strict building regulations? The answer lies in their size: houses that are less than 120 square feet (11 square meters) are not regarded as dwelling units under the International Building Code (IBC). They slip under the wire, and can be built in a few days, perhaps over a weekend by volunteers, church groups, high school students, apprentice or vocational training programs, or neighbors.

Having heard a critical view of the Tiny House Village, in Seattle, we decided we would like to see it for ourselves. LIHI was most helpful in finding a way for us to visit, while remaining unobtrusive and respectful of the people living there.

When we arrived, we were met by Bob who offered us "the tour." A quiet man, he showed us the little homes and talked about how being there had given him a chance to get his life together. He showed us the communal kitchen, showers, and bathrooms, and let us into an empty "home." It was stark and unoccupied, which revealed just how small these houses are, as a result of the building restrictions. There is a window and enough room for a bed and some shelves.

Bob explained that he and tidying up don't go together, so he didn't invite us into his own tiny house, but he did point out the Californian poppies he'd planted and another little porch that had also been decorated with plants. He says his house is insulated "a bit."

We were also lucky enough to meet Jerry, a young woman who has one of the larger and better-built tiny houses, where her deaf son can visit and stay with her. Located at the top of the site, Jerry's is a black, timber-clad house. Inside there is a raised bed with a "tunnel" underneath for storage and space for her son to play and sleep. There are also plenty of shelves. Jerry's son does not live with her permanently because, she says, he can get a better education living with his grandmother.

The tiny homes were built by apprentices, with the help of the church and other groups. For example, Jerry's house was built by Sawhorse Revolution. The Sawhorse Revolution works with students on projects, helping them to think about education, construction, and working in new ways through all aspects of the development and design of various building projects. Jerry likes the fact that her house faces the fence, which gives her more privacy. She and her dog, which she is looking

ABOVE The kitchens are located in a canvas-covered area that has food-storage and cooking facilities for the village residents. This is a sociable space where the residents can meet and support each other.

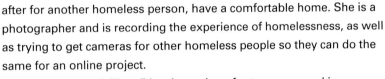

OPPOSITE At the entrance to the village is a reception hut staffed by project workers or residents, to protect the site from strangers and provide a welcome for visitors.

RIGHT These little homes are quite basic, with room for a bed and shelves, but being able to lock the doors and feel safe is very important.

BELOW Jerry looks after a homeless friend's dog. Her larger, better-designed house means that her son can come and stay.

after for another homeless person, have a comfortable home. She is a photographer and is recording the experience of homelessness, as well as trying to get cameras for other homeless people so they can do the same for an online project.

This particular "village" has been there for two years and is more secure for the future because it is on land owned by, and has the support of, the Lutheran Church of the Good Shepherd. This will, hopefully, give the project a chance to develop grass-root initiatives that will involve residents in making it more comfortable and installing better facilities. A group called Nickelsville helps to facilitate the running of the village, representing the residents and interfacing with LIHI about the needs of the village.

People that live in the village have been made homeless through many unfortunate and tragic circumstances. For example, Lionel, another resident, is there because he can only be treated for his diabetes on Medicaid, which he says is better in Seattle than in his previous city. As Bob says, "It is touching meeting everyone new to the place. We all bring our own stuff. We are a close group of strangers thrown together. It's OK." The village has a no drugs or drink policy, which adds to the safety of those living there.

Bob adds, "These places are the future for homeless people—it is a start." Before we left, an older woman came by and echoed the friendliness, saying, "Welcome to our village."

There are thousands of homeless people living in Seattle and huge social problems in the city. The housing provided for them needs to be better. The homeless people living in Seattle's Tiny House Village represent just a handful, but they are a handful of people who appreciate what they have.

ABOVE Linda and Antje built their contemporary home above and behind a garage where a workshop had once been. Although their home is on the edge of a Conservation Area, they only had to retain the roofline.

Linda and Antje already had connections with Cromer, in Suffolk, England, and were looking for a project. They spotted an old workshop, which looked as if it was on a pretty good plot. Luckily, it was available to buy. It had been for sale with planning permission, which Linda and Antje "tweaked" to their own design with the help of their builder. One requirement of the planning permission was the need for level access through the garage and into the house and courtyard. In the courtyard they installed timber flooring using scaffolding boards, which were wide, rough, and treated with anti-slip oil.

Linda and Antje created the inviting courtyard themselves. They say that they did as much of the work as they could, but it wasn't a complete "self-build." It is their favorite part of the home; they especially enjoy sitting there in the mornings for

breakfast. The walls of the courtyard are painted white and the rooflines of the surrounding buildings are visible beyond. Linda and Antje love the convenience of being located in the town.

Previously, the workshop had been a dry storeroom in a timber yard, some of which is gone, and next door were other workshops and a carpenters' yard. They met a local whose father once ran a Rifle Club there and, indeed, Linda and Antje found some old paper targets.

Situated on the edge of a Conservation Area, their tiny house might have been contentious as a modern conversion, but "everyone down here likes it" and there are friendly comments from the locals. They explain, "We used local Norfolk red and yellow bricks, and really enjoyed getting the shades and order of the bricks right by laying them out to get the right blend." They had to mix

"We did every single thing in the courtyard ourselves... it is our favorite bit. It gets the sun in the morning and is a great place to sit for coffee and breakfast surrounded by pots of plants."

in a few new bricks, as they couldn't find quite enough recycled ones for the build. The upper level of the house is clad in white, which wasn't in the original design, but the planners agreed to the fresher paint. The success of the building lies in its mixture of architecture, planning, coming up with solutions, and careful sourcing of materials such as bricks, floorboards, courtyard scaffolding boards, and other recycled materials.

According to Linda and Antje, "It was a lot of work." The delivery of the various materials and access only through the garage "was a nightmare." The builder commented that he wanted to work "down a lane next time!"

The garage doors are recycled 1950s folding doors, which came from Wales. Linda says, "I learnt about fixings and joins, etc. I love meeting old skilled people." One of these people was a carpenter who could do "anything in wood." He had worked on tall ships. Another was a man who came up with structural solutions for the steel frame for the roof, which had to be staggered so as not to change the roofline. They went down the structural engineer route and got tangled up in the minutiae

BELOW A level access beside the garage leads to a large courtyard with pots of plants and white walls. This provides a pretty outdoor eating area. The kitchen-diner has large glass doors, giving an open feel to the space.

ABOVE The stairs behind the garage lead to the spacious bedroom and compact sitting room at the top of the building.

of regulations. Looking back, they believe that they could have avoided these if they had found their builder earlier, as he had the "can-do" knowledge to make the structure.

To get the height they wanted in the rooms, they needed to put in fire-retardant panels and work with the two triangular steel structures that give the building its striking staggered roofline. As the roof elevation changes, the ceilings get lower and, past the bathroom, there's a step down into the small sitting room at the front of the house. They put a large window in the sitting room, closely following the outline of the front elevation to design the shape and to maximize light (see page 10, center left).

The interior is minimalist in style, with no extraneous clutter. There is a kitchen-diner downstairs, which has large glass doors that open out onto the courtyard. There is good storage and wooden countertops, plus a refrigerator for cold drinks on summer days.

"Wherever you look, there are windows and a new view. At night, the beam from the lighthouse can be seen as it swings round. We have started to enjoy our relaxation time here. It is all still very new... We can walk anywhere: to the beach, along the coastal path, and to the cinema—anywhere."

Upstairs there is a good-sized bedroom, with reclaimed natural wooden floorboards that were obtained from an old police station, and a high ceiling. There is a mezzanine, but it can't be used for sleeping, so the steps leading up to it are on a pulley system to discourage guests from trying to climb up.

LEFT The bedroom is open to the roofline, giving a sense of space and light. There is also a useful balcony area served by retractable steps, which provides extra space for storing belongings.

RIGHT Upstairs, between the bedroom and the light, airy sitting room, is a corridor with a door to the shower room. The sitting room has a large vaulted window that overlooks the street outside and is furnished simply to add to the sense of space.

Loraine's husband Selwyn bought Baldry's Yard in England's Norfolk in 1980. Baldry's Yard was once an old malt house for the Young Chawser Young Brewery and was in ruins at the time. The yard included a large, white house where Loraine and Selwyn lived before Loraine downsized into an apartment above the workshop building opposite the white house. Part of the brewery's history can be found in the workshop beneath the apartment in the form of an old well or liquor pond, which was once used by the brewery.

The building to the front of Baldry's Yard was once an old counting house, where the men from the malt house were paid before, as rumor has it, going straight to the pub to spend their earnings. A bottle of "Jack Baldry" was found at the site and lives on a shelf in Loraine's room. The counting house is now a café and the Backspace a place for workshops and other events.

While the White House needed a little renovation, the workshop was a place of squalor and there were also a few old sheds and a garage. The workshop had no floor and was open to the roof—it was the last "shed" still in need of renovation after Selwyn died.

Selwyn was a great supporter of homeless and out-of-work people in the area. He provided a roof over their heads and they adored him.

ABOVE The entrance to Loraine's flat is the door of the old workshop in the small courtyard behind the Backspace, a place where classes such as yoga and drumming take place.

OPPOSITE Baldry's Yard is comprised of a long row of buildings that have been converted into homes behind the old counting house, which is now the Angel Café.

> "I've never actually wanted more rooms or space since moving here. I have no need for a garden, as we can have family picnics on our land... My mission was to simplify my life and make it smaller."

With the "help of the troops," including some of the people Selwyn supported, he rebuilt much of Baldry's Yard and transformed the buildings into homes. Their children helped clean the bricks to build the walls. As Loraine says, "There was a lot of jolly unpaid work."

When Selwyn died, Loraine moved into a small cottage behind the White House and this was then rented out. This resulted in the old workshop becoming a refuge for much of her stuff, including her piano.

ABOVE The view from the balcony shows the sitting and kitchen-diner areas, as well as Loraine's cozy bedroom. It is the height of the beamed roof that gives her home its sense of space and light.

Loraine found an architect "with a brilliant brain" to help her design her new apartment above the workshop. The design included the magnificent beams, some of which had to be moved to make the space practical. In places the beams also serve as an open divider between the living and sleeping areas. The floor is made from wide oak floorboards from Loraine's old cottage, which Loraine wanted to remind her of her old home. The balcony remains to be finished one day.

Loraine was able to move into her apartment in 2010. Although it is small, the door is nearly always open to family and friends, and Loraine need only go next door to the white house for her tai chi and drumming. The café is also there for coffee or a meal when she doesn't feel like cooking.

There are plenty of windows in the apartment and also windows in the roof. The latter, along with the high ceilings, give the apartment a feeling of more space and light than there really is. The walls are white and hung with Loraine's favorite paintings. She is especially fond of one of the paintings by Ray Humphrey and on the bedroom wall is a portrait of the artist himself. Loraine's furniture is comfortable and the kitchen-diner has a sociable round table and bookshelves. There is another bookshelf on the landing and an African djembe and dundunba for playing with friends or practicing on alone.

BELOW A semi-divide of old beams marks out the living and sleeping areas, while large Velux windows throw light into the conversion.

The Findhorn Foundation, in Forres, Scotland, was once a trailer (caravan) park before becoming the thriving internationally renowned intentional community looking at new ways of living, working, and being that it is today. There is still a trailer park (Findhorn Bay Holiday Park) next door, which means you can obtain licences for caravans. There are a few caravans nestled in the woods adjoining one of the roads within the Foundation Village, two of which are now tiny homes built on long trailer (caravan) bases. One of these ecomobile homes belongs to **Graham** and is called "Eucalyptus," a tree that can be seen from the long window in the bedroom. Graham organizes conferences at the Findhorn Foundation, while his experience as an architect means he can provide design solutions for some of Findhorn's buildings. His principles include "voluntary simplicity" and "anti-materialism." For Graham, how he lives and works is a political act.

The journey begins at the start of the path leading down to the ecomobile. Graham regards this raised wooden path with its overhead structure as part and parcel of his home and surroundings—with the plants being part of the journey to the front door. The entrance is a light-filled glass porch, which contains four large pots of luscious

ABOVE The pathway leading to Graham's minimalist home in the trees is part of a journey of meaning. Everything, from the planting to the raised pathway, has meaning as you approach the large entrance.

OPPOSITE This view down the path from the entrance is from the porch terrace, which has large glazed doors shaded by plants that will eventually cover the pergola.

OVERLEAF The porch area is full of light and acts as a conservatory for Graham's large, sculptural pot plants, as well as somewhere for his shoes, hats, and scarves.

THE FINDHORN FOUNDATION

A Scottish charitable trust, The Findhorn Foundation was registered in 1972 by members of the Findhorn Ecovillage, a dynamic spiritual community located in the Moray Firth, in northern Scotland, and one of the largest intentional communities in the UK. The Findhorn Ecovillage was originally founded in 1962 by Eileen Caddy and her second husband, Peter, along with their friend Dorothy Maclean. All three were determined to follow a disciplined personal path, guided by the inner spirit and the natural world. The Foundation now has international standing and provides inspiration for those looking to follow an eco-friendly and sustainable approach to living, as well as providing environmental and spiritual workshops and courses.

ABOVE This uncluttered circular room is beautifully designed to provide sitting, eating, and cooking areas. There is a large wood-burning stove for warmth. There is no TV, washing machine, dishwasher, or microwave. Graham, like others in the Findhorn community, uses the communal laundry.

sculptural plants and shelving units for storing shoes—
this is the place for "shoes-off."

The octagonal center of the home rests partially on
the old trailer base and is a room of light and white. For
Graham, light is the most important aspect of his home
and he has designed the building to let in maximum
natural light. There is nothing extraneous. As Graham
says, "I'm a bit OCD."

The "roundness" of this room, which combines the
kitchen and sitting areas, is both open and nurturing.
Although in a shared space, neither the kitchen nor living
areas intrude on each other. Graham has a minimalist
esthetic, with the decorative details being provided by
nature, which can easily be seen through the unadorned
windows. To him, architraves equal "clutter." He says,
"I'm a modernist." The kitchen takes up about a third of
this open area and is free of clutter. There are chairs, a
sofa, a bookshelf, and a few paintings, including two
Aboriginal paintings, which were gifts from his daughter.
There's also a large, intricate Zulu basket, the shape of
which is enhanced by being placed next to a white wall.

There is a bamboo floor throughout, which is
beautiful, sustainable, and hardwearing. It provides
continuity between the different living spaces. Cleverly,
Graham has also used this material for the windowsills
and countertops.

From the central octagonal room there is a link-way
through to the bedroom. Cupboards run along its length
on one side and there's a bathroom on the other. The
bathroom cabinet does not intrude because Graham has
recessed it into the wall. The link-way roof is made from
a double layer of polycarbonate, which can be lit from
behind, so light is diffused by day and night along the
length of the space joining the two rooms.

The bedroom is a "sacred space" and also kept very
simple. There is the long window, with its view of the
eucalyptus, and a wide window at the top of the wall
opposite the bed for star-gazing. There are shades
(blinds) to mitigate the long, light summer evenings of
the north of Scotland.

BELOW At the far end of the building is the bedroom with its long window. This gives a view of the eucalyptus tree, after which the house is named, and also the woods.

Chapter two

ON THE WATER

People who live on or near water love the views, the nature, the changing seasons, and the story each day tells from dawn till dusk. Some live in cities, as is the case with the owners of the two houseboats on Lake Union, right in the middle of Seattle, which feature in this chapter. This lake is an oasis of hugely varying houseboats and floating homes. Some are super-huge and some tiny. In Seattle, as in any city, people live on rivers, canals, and lakes. In the UK, more than 30,000 people live in this way. Their homes are not necessarily tiny or affordable, but allow them to move or moor permanently, and sometimes create their own special communities.

Sally's bright yellow floating home is hidden behind a fence, along with others, in a private mooring, giving her a beautiful place to live on one of the shores of Lake Union, while Linda and Kevin's houseboat is not so much "tiny" as "tiny for them," having moved from a large property on land.

The two barges that feature in this chapter are both Dutch barges which were brought over from the Netherlands and converted on the Norfolk and Suffolk shores. While Muriel and Alan have created a static house on water, the very much smaller barge that Lee acquired is a labor of love and a reflection of her determination to complete as much of the build as possible herself. Lee found materials and design solutions that enable her to move her home whenever she wants.

Then there are those who love to live by the water, such as Sibylle in the north of Scotland, whose home has huge expanses of glass framing an ever-changing sea and sky. Everything is about the view.

Lee's boat is moored in the Blackwater Estuary, in Maldon, Essex. Maldon is a small, thriving town, and the second oldest town in the English county of Essex. Through a jumble of boatyard chains and launch lines down toward boats, both small and large, looms a beautiful 102-ft (31-m) brigantine square-rigged ship called "The Lady of Avenel." As we approach, people are working on deck to ready her for the high tide. She is moored by a wooden walkway and nestled next to her is Lee's Dutch barge.

Lee's dream of living on a narrow boat was inspired early on in life when she worked in Westminster, London, 35 years ago. While traveling for her job, she saw the narrow boats on the Regent's Canal and her dream took hold. However, it wasn't until her parents died and her children had grown up that she had the freedom and independence to realize her dream in 2005. As Lee says, "It was a question of now or never and I did it!"

Lee bought the barge, which is a Boier Aak, in the Netherlands when it was just an empty hull. It had been an eel barge on the River Rhine in the past. The engine was disconnected from the steering. It was impossible to bring the barge to the UK by sea, so it was loaded onto a lorry and ferried home.

RIGHT The wheelhouse still serves its original working function, but is also a sitting room with built-in storage below the seats and floor.

Lee decided to do virtually all the renovation work, from joinery to welding and upholstery. Her plans for the barge were envisioned right from the start and she says, "I more or less stuck to my plan." The local men in the pub thought she couldn't do it and some were dismissive, so her success has made her very proud of her achievements. All the original portholes had to be removed and replaced with new glass and brass handles. The framing of the portholes posed a problem, as they were all at different angles, and there were a few times when Lee decided to call in a carpenter.

BELOW Lee's Dutch barge was transported by lorry from the Netherlands, as it wasn't seaworthy. She transformed this jolly green boat into a modern home without changing its character.

The wheelhouse doubles as a sitting room. Every spare inch is used for storage—even the broom cupboard is located under the floor. It is a wonderfully light space, with glass all around providing a view out. The upholstered seating and cozy cushions belie the practicality of the space, with the adjacent steering wheel and controls being ready for any trip Lee might wish to take. As Lee says, "I like the idea of being able to take off. The small size of the boat means I can travel alone." To enhance the space below deck, Lee moved the steering-wheel casing in order to make room for a tiny bathroom.

A short flight of wooden steps leads down to the main living room and kitchen below deck. In practical terms, the walls of the downstairs area are insulated with wooden paneling that is fixed to welded supports. Lee used Earthwool® on the curved walls. Ever with an eye for saving money, Lee bought the oak veneered flooring that runs throughout the downstairs of the barge from a local businessman—and got it for half price.

Downstairs, there is every sense of the smallness of the space being belied by clever storage solutions and minimalism. Each tread of the wooden steps, for example, is hinged to provide a space inside the step for hiding Lee's belongings. Lee also took the back legs off her blue sofa

ABOVE As you step down onto the deck of the barge from the walkway, you find the entrance to the wheelhouse, which leads down some stairs to a very well-designed little kitchen, tiny bathroom, and sitting room.

so that it could be recessed into the sloping sides of the barge. The only other furniture is a matching blue armchair and traditional chest of drawers that Lee has had for years.

The kitchen area is sleek and tidy. Tucked in beside the kitchen units is a useful wire storage unit, which was once an old workmen's locker. Each shelf is small, so there is no space for stuff to rattle around, and rods also stop the doors opening when the boat is on the move. Cleverly, the shelves in the living area are made of box crates that can be turned round in order to stop things falling out. There's a built-in oven recessed into the wall, while the kitchen surface has a built-in stovetop. The kitchen countertops came from a science laboratory in an old school and the drawers on both sides of the units are short for practical reasons. A door behind the kitchen units leads to a convenient shower and loo, with an ingenious herb rack fixed to the back of the door to hold Lee's lotions and potions.

Surprisingly, the bedroom, which at the front of the boat, also has an enormous chest of drawers along the wall, but this only fitted in with the top and bottom taken off. This room is calm and peaceful, with the curves of paneling and fabrics transforming it into a relaxing retreat. To enhance the light and keep the grain of the wood in the bedroom, Lee treated the paneling with a white polish, creating a lime-washed effect.

ABOVE The kitchen area, along with the rest of the boat, is designed for living well while being on the move. There is clever storage, including some shelving that was once an old workshop locker, to keep everything from rattling around or falling.

"It's cozy and really adequate for my needs. I'm not a materialist and living simply makes my life easy."

BELOW The bedroom is in the curved hull at the front of the boat. White polish has been used to soften the color of the wood-paneled walls.

Lee has fulfilled her dream of living on the water. In her soothing estuary retreat, her love for, and affinity with, water is enhanced by the shifts and changes of the sea and weather, as well as by the constantly changing landscape of boats as they come and go with the ebb and flow of the tides.

Muriel and Alan bought their Dutch barge in 1984 and it has a plate that dates it at 1904. The Dutch barge "traded anything"—as long as it was what they described as "clean cargo." They were able to bring the 80-ft (24-m) long barge over from the Netherlands and now live in it in a marina in Norfolk, England. They decided to gut and renovate it completely. At first, when their children were young, it was only used as a holiday home. Then, 15 years ago, they decided to refurbish it as their main home. Muriel explains that they have always liked narrow boats and the idea of roaming the inland waterways. Their barge, though, is static and in a legal residential berth in a marina with other boats, most of which are smaller. They describe an anomaly that if they were traveling they would be subject to VAT (Value Added Tax), but no UK Council Tax, but, as they are permanent in the marina, the converse is true.

Faults such as condensation, which had been acceptable when the barge was only a holiday home, had to be corrected. So, they insulated the barge with 4in (10cm) of polyurethane, built a timber frame, and put in a second layer of insulation once they'd decided on the layout they wanted. "We felt confident, as we had done this type of renovation before in houses."

Starting again meant they were able to build an energy-efficient home that costs half of what their "normal" house cost. They have a multi-fuel Parkray Stove and only need an additional 2-kilowatt heater in winter. Finding their cooker was a "saga," but they eventually found ex-catering ones for sale at a very reasonable price.

ABOVE LEFT The wheel of the Dutch barge is on the aft deck, where a small door leading down steep steps belies the spaciousness of the living accommodation below.

OPPOSITE AND OVERLEAF Muriel and Alan's relatively large Dutch barge is designed to stay moored in its static berth on the Norfolk coast. From 1904, it traded in "clean" cargoes until it became redundant. The barge sits in a marina surrounded by other boats, some of which can set off across the Norfolk waterways.

LEFT Behind the kitchen and leading to the bedrooms is a door disguised as a bookshelf. The central painting lifts up to become a star-studded cover for the rooflight above.

The living area is divided into two levels, which are accessed via steps down from the deck. On the first level is the dining area, which doubles as an office, and, from there, there are more steps down to Muriel's artist's studio. Once the Captain's quarters, the studio is where Muriel works with acrylics, oils, and pastels, as well as sewing. It's wood-lined with a custom-built worktop made to fit the curve of the barge's bow. The ceiling is low, but, as she is sitting at her work, this suits her fine. Her sewing machine is at the ready and artists' materials, thread, and scissors are at hand.

Muriel and Alan bought old floorboards for some of the floors in the boat. These are layered over polystyrene blocks, then water-resistant chipboard. The sitting-room floor is covered with a traditional "Persian" carpet and rugs. Most of the walls are painted white, apart from the rich red of the living room, with its comfortable sofa and chairs. The portholes have been framed and use one of the windows to good effect to show off a favorite stained-glass panel.

Although they say their "house on water" is not that tiny, they still had to downsize and get rid of a lot of possessions when they moved in. This was hard for Muriel and, as she says, "It felt awful." Alan is not as emotional about their possessions, but they were able to bring a few beloved pieces of furniture and sentimental or beautiful belongings such as paintings. Muriel used to run an art gallery and there are stacks of paintings she hasn't the heart to let go.

The kitchen has swing doors, which gives it a feeling of the Wild West. They particularly like the hatch on the kitchen ceiling, which their children painted with a night sky and stars. Beyond the kitchen, at the other end of the barge, is their sumptuous bedroom with ensuite bathroom. There is also a very small bedroom with "bunk beds, which were the children's before they grew up."

Although they have no intention of moving, they could, if they didn't like the neighbors. Alan quips, "When the floods come, we can take our boat with us." Living on the water brings nature and wildlife right up to their home. They are immersed in the changing weather. As Alan says, "Only a north-westerly is capable of rocking this boat."

ABOVE Muriel has a tiny space under the foredeck for her hobbies, where she can paint and draw, and get out her sewing machine.

OPPOSITE The stairs from the living room, next to the wood-burning stove, lead to a study area where Muriel and Alan's Chicago Cottage Organ, which they brought from Maldon, in Essex, takes pride of place.

Sally's colorful yellow floating home is called "Pecheboutier," a name she came across when she was on vacation in France. It was the name of a painting she bought by a local French artist (whose identity is unknown). Sally's home is on Lake Union, in Seattle, and is hidden behind a fence along with other homes reached down some steps to a walkway. The entrance is a covered porch with some colorful pots of flowers and there's a curved red roof. Sally lives there with her dog, Eleanor. She finds living on the water "simple, yet challenging." Her houseboat will stay put, because Sally took the motor out. As she comments, "I don't want to go anywhere."

Sally comes from Ohio originally, where her father was a shipbuilder. She has an affinity for water and, along with her then husband, was on the lookout for a houseboat to live on. Having worked in the past as a molecular biologist on the human genome and then in the food industry, Sally is now enjoying the freedom the houseboat gives her to undertake consultation work from a hidden office opposite the little bathroom.

"Pecheboutier" was found in a dry dock, with a new aluminum hull being fitted, and Sally felt that a floating home was somewhere she could afford. A local builder, Bill Haggard, had built the houseboat. He was the father of Riley Haggard. Riley still focuses on Northwest Modern architectural influences and, as Sally says, "You can truly see the passion that goes into each and every home that is built." Sally explains, "A lot of the home was original." Indeed, it was the beveled glass windows, which Sally loves, that decided the sale.

Sally brought a pink armchair and two antique lights with her to the houseboat. The galley kitchen came from "a very old building" and Sally believes the table and

PREVIOUS PAGES Sally's houseboat is in a small private marina on Lake Union. Its bright yellow, timber façade pops with color against the surrounding boats.

RIGHT Sally's dog sleeps in the kitchen/living room, which makes the most of the contrast between the warm wood and the rich furnishings in pinks and reds.

chairs date from the time of the American Civil War. The age and style of the houseboat encourage Sally to use her best Donegal china dishes every day and drink water from champagne glasses. The kitchen area has wooden countertops and also a "pantry" with shelves for cans and other stores. On the other side of this living area are bench seats and tables, with a spot on the floor for Eleanor. There is plenty of storage under the bench seats, which Sally has had reupholstered.

The bathroom tiles were made from recycled crushed glass in "the colors of the Adriatic" by Bedrock Industries, in Seattle, who specialize in using 100 percent recycled glass in their products. The shelving and cupboards in the bathroom are made from the original warm-colored wood, which contrasts beautifully with the modern green tiles. The bathroom window has beveled glass and Sally believes that this is the only example of this type of window on Lake Union. The windows are "leaded" throughout and also beveled, adding to the originality of Sally's home.

Sally added another level to the houseboat to make room for a lofty bedroom, with views across the lake. The addition was built "as a shed" offsite and then a crane lifted the new room on top of the houseboat. Sally admits, "I didn't want to watch." The bedroom is reached via a stepladder up to a deck with a deckchair from where Sally can enjoy her surroundings. An overhang protects her from the weather. She has total blackout shades (blinds) to keep out the light on long summer days. At the time, the laws regarding how much added floor space was allowed were not as strict, so Sally was able to build a good-sized bedroom. She says that having the pink armchair from her old home "makes all the difference" and she also enjoys her Mister Johnson Art Deco light.

"My neighbors all help each other and it's a tight-knit community… Living on my floating home is such an adventure… I feel younger—wilder."

One of Sally's paintings is a joint work of art with Terry Heckler, who designed the Starbucks logo and now runs a not-for-profit organization, Cranory, which supports veterans through creativity and working with artists to aid their recovery. Sally is helping with this work and their collaborative artwork hangs above her bed. Terry has never been able to stop creating and, over and above his corporate work, has continued to make art. He has always drawn with crayons at hand, finding that this "is very stress-reducing and helps my problem-solving."

Sally wants to replace the stepladder up to the bedroom with proper stairs, but, as the boat needs repainting in "geranium and yellow," the stairs have to wait for the moment. For this reason, Eleanor, her old dog, has to sleep downstairs as she cannot climb up the stepladder. There were already speakers throughout "Pecheboutier," so she installed some upstairs for that all-round music experience. For the brave, there is a wooden bench on the roof.

BELOW Sally added another level to the houseboat. This gives her great views over Lake Union from the terrace, which has an overhang to shelter her from the weather.

This houseboat is a "movable feast." Powered by paddles, it has moved 12 times to different locations on the oasis of Seattle's Lake Union.

The first question you ask on seeing **Kevin and Linda's** houseboat is, "Is this really a tiny home?" But the houseboat is a massive change from their large house in Seattle so, for them, it's relative. They moved from a house of 4,000 square feet (372 square meters) to a houseboat of 1,200 square feet (112 square meters) on the "waterfront where you can put your toes in."

Kevin runs a realty company selling houseboats and floating homes. He and Linda had been coming down to their own houseboat on Lake Union at the weekends for some time until one day, 12 years ago, they decided they didn't want to leave. As Linda asked at the time, "Why are we going home?"

After the decision to leave their Seattle house, they found it refreshing to get rid of stuff—"What a liberating thing it is!" Buying clothes in their new space has a system: one in, one out. The only must-haves from their old house were "Amigo" the parrot and Kevin's mother's collection of Japanese fishing floats. As Linda says, "Life is better when you own it."

Kevin and Linda's new home is a houseboat, which means it is connected but can be moved. (Floating homes, in contrast, are more permanently fixed in their berths.) Being able to move their boat means that they can switch to another berth if they need to. Kevin adds that the slips "are like parking spaces."

"Everyone joins in and puts up Christmas lights on all the boats and a choir on one of them wanders about the lake singing good cheer."

Modern mooring platforms tend to be made from aluminum, which looks good and lasts.

All the houseboats and floating homes that are located on Lake Union are owned. Many are wonderfully creative and colorful homes on the water. Kevin and Linda have moved their boat 12 times, which is "different, but not difficult."

Kevin and Linda have just refurbished their houseboat. Linda comments, "When we found it, it was horrid and dirty. No one else would have wanted to buy it." Clearly, for them, the challenge of turning the houseboat into a beautiful home was not too daunting and they set about it with real enthusiasm. They have designed their new home for comfort and style.

ABOVE Kevin and Linda have completely renovated the "horrid and dirty" houseboat to make it a contemporary and comfortable home with lots of entertaining space.

Downstairs there's a large sitting/
dining room and an open galley kitchen.
Kevin is particularly fond of his LED
lighting, set into a fake beam above the
countertop. He can change the colors
with a gadget according to their mood...
tonight, perhaps, a sunset? There are
other LED lights throughout the
houseboat, which Kevin can dim at will
with his iPhone. The ceiling is made of
"saw-marked wood to give a rough
beechwood effect and then whitewashed
to enhance the grain." Kevin says it
creates a "nautical, beachy look!" They
designed every detail themselves,
including a must-have for the kitchen—
the dark red Verona cooking range.

Beyond the sitting room is a large,
black-and-white-themed deck for
morning coffees, informal meals, and
social events. Kevin can play music
anywhere in their home from his handy
gadget—as loud or as quiet as they want
without disturbing the neighbors. This is
a party boat!

Under the floor in the kitchen area,
there's room for lots of storage, including
all their vacation stuff.

RIGHT The new kitchen has
a whitewashed ceiling and
plenty of lighting, including a
LED system above the galley
countertop. They can control
this with a special gadget to
change the color to suit
different moods.

ABOVE Kevin and Linda are especially pleased with their newly decorated bathroom, with its soft gray walls, white trim and towels, and granite countertop. There is a decorative white mermaid and a "porthole" mirrored bathroom cabinet.

Upstairs is the bathroom, a guest room, and their bedroom. Kevin and Linda are particularly proud of the new bathroom with its granite top and twin sinks. The "porthole mirror" conceals their bathroom cabinet and a white mermaid ornament against the soft gray walls sets the tone for the color scheme. There is also a merman made from tin cans by a man in Haiti and mermaid hooks. They have a large rain shower and underfloor heating.

The white and soft gray color scheme extends into their bedroom, where the white wrought-iron bed is dressed with soft white pillows and a quilted bedcover. Darker gray curtains obscure the closet and double glass doors that lead to their own private deck at the stern of the boat.

Between the bathroom and the bedroom is a spiral staircase leading to the wheelhouse and another topside deck with the best views. It is yet again a place for people to gather and enjoy the hospitality of this larger-than-life couple. There are lights strung across the deck and all around are the twinkling lights of other boats and the city beyond.

Kevin says that when the weather is hot he leaps into the lake from this great height. He says it's safe with only ducks, geese, and other waterfowl on the lake, although eagles can sometimes be seen soaring above if they are lucky.

Kevin and Linda enjoy everything more in their lake home, including seeing their friends and going to events. They adore the lake with its constantly changing scenery, the weather on the water, and also huge events such as the Christmas Boat Parade. For this event, the boats are decorated with Christmas lights and a choir performs on one of the boats. In 2008 they had the Grand Finale right in front of Kevin and Linda's houseboat. "It was spectacular!"

Most of the surrounding dwellings have been built on the lake, but new rules say that no more water residences can be built there, so people have to buy existing houseboats and floating homes to renovate and remodel, or add one-time-allowed additional square footage. It is possible to move to another marina, but who would want to?

RIGHT A spiral staircase leads up to the wheelhouse and a generous deck that gives Kevin and Linda yet another party area, with deck furniture, colored lights, and a lakeside view.

Sibylle lives in a little house on the shores of an estuary north of Forres, in the north of Scotland. Sibylle had always wanted to live by the water. She is a voice therapist and psychotherapist, as well as a naturopath and teacher of meditation. She has also worked in theater. Sibylle admits to being "a lapsed musician and artist" and her tambura sits in the living room. She uses this instrument in her voice therapy workshops. As Sibylle explains, " I sing to it and it is easy to play."

Sibylle had begun running workshops in the community at the nearby Findhorn Foundation village (see page 34). The more often she came up to Findhorn, the more friends she made, and she began to come earlier and leave later. Then she saw the cottage on the estuary for sale and made an offer. It took a total of five attempts to buy the cottage, as the owner kept wavering. After the fourth attempt, Sibylle decided to buy a property at the Findhorn Foundation village instead.

When her parents died, however, everything began to move in her direction and she was finally able to get the owner of the cottage to sell at the fifth attempt. "The thought of living by the water and being part of a community was what I wanted… it was time." Looking after her parents had taken her to the edge of exhaustion and she needed this

"If I were to move, I would want to take the house and the view with me. Community is important to me, too. I don't think it's healthy to live in isolation."

OPPOSITE The bay views can be enjoyed from the deck above the garden, which leads down to the shore, as the tides, seasons, and weather change from hour to hour and day to day.

BELOW The wide expanse of glass enables Sibylle to watch the sunset and her peaceful surroundings all year round in the sitting room.

healing view of the water below the horizon constantly rippling, moving, and changing color with the seasons, tides, and weather. Sibylle elaborates, "I was so burnt out I couldn't even meditate, but, as I looked at the horizon and the water, everything calmed down. Sunsets in the north of Scotland are different in the summer and winter, as the shortest winter days turn into the longest summer days when, Sibylle says, "You can read the paper at midnight."

Fortunately, Sibylle was able to sell her new house at the Findhorn Foundation at a good price and, at last, could buy the cottage on the "bay." The whole process took five long years. At one time, the cottage had been a corrugated iron shed used for boat-building. It had no insulation and not much between a basic floor and the beach below.

One of the previous owners had built breeze-block walls around the corrugated iron and put in windows but, for Sibylle, the whole place needed remodeling. The house was divided into three rooms, with a teeny porch with a very small toilet on one side and two cooker plates on the other. The whole place had been truly tiny. Although the cottage had been extended to provide a hallway, kitchen, and bathroom by the time it came into Sibylle's possession, it was all too boxy and so she set about taking down walls and working with a builder to completely open up the view to the bay.

Not only did the builders find corrugated tin in the walls, but also that some of the carpeted floor was only suspended on joists above the sand and pebbles. So they doubled the joists and put in "double bubble and aluminum" insulation before covering this with board and flooring. As Sibylle points out, "I now have a level floor." Sibylle also built an extension at the back of the cottage so that she could install a good bathroom.

The garden runs down a slope of sand and pebbles to the seawall, so Sibylle designed a veranda to sit on. Three Scot's pines belonging to a neighbor grow next to the veranda. Sibylle loves looking at these trees; the only downside is that the shade they cast restricts her ability to use solar panels.

RIGHT Between the kitchen and the curved extension is an adaptable space that can be used as a studio, work area, or dining space.

The wooden floor is recycled and the marble under the wood-burning stove is reclaimed. Sibylle's wood for the stove comes mainly from the beach, as it is washed down the rivers and surrounding land onto the sand with the rise and fall of the tides. The repeated action of sun and water seasons the wood, so it burns clean. The rivers flowing into the bay dilute the seawater. A friend of Sibylle's has "a passion for foraging" and he loves to pick up driftwood, even though he doesn't have a wood-burner himself. Sibylle insists on paying him for the wood. The same friend also supplies all the kindling she needs. Another friend chops up the wood for her and, again, she pays him—so, nearly free.

The sitting area has a wonderful hexagonal ceiling, with the seating set into the bay window. She was determined to retain the beautiful vista and the windows enhance the breadth of the view that gives Sibylle so much pleasure. As Sibylle explains, "It's all about the view." The bedroom also has wide views, which take in all weathers, times of day, and seasons. At low tide the sky is reflected in the muddy ripples of the exposed shore and the sunsets are spectacular.

Sibylle has made a peaceful and comfortable home that reflects her creative life. And she goes on to say, "I am grateful every day."

OPPOSITE The living room, which is edged with white upholstered seating with lots of plump cushions, provides a comfortable living and social space. The white walls reflect the light that streams in through the windows.

BELOW The bedroom is a very simple room, with a view out to the pine trees and beyond to the beautiful bay.

RIGHT Tidal water and wind mean Sibylle can get much of her wood for the stove from the beach—a free resource that is especially pleasurable.

Chapter three
ON WHEELS

The tiny-house-on-wheels movement is massive in the USA and beginning to flourish around the world. These clever little houses are designed to provide everything you might need, including a kitchen sink. The designs, which feature very clever storage and multifunctional furniture, make living in this way possible.

There is some debate about what constitutes "tiny." Tiny houses built on lorry-chassis wheelbases are defined by the sizes in which they come and also by height, which means that many of the occupants sleep in loft areas with low ceilings. Alexis and Brian had just moved into their tiny home on wheels in a forest when we visited, and had loved the design process and making it their own.

Many tiny-home builders have turned designing and building tiny homes for others into a business, working with the owners to ensure the build reflects their preferred design and ergonomic needs. For example, Carmen and Tom's home was specifically built for this tall family, while Mari's home needed to be accessible to meet her physical needs. Hannah is one of those tiny homers who has turned designer-builder and also challenged the zoning laws and other restrictions that face owners.

Then there are trucks, lorries, and vans, all providing homes in fields and cities. Some of these, such as Gosia's Polish-inspired home and Emma's lorry retreat, are unprepossessing from the outside, but beautifully furnished and decorated inside.

Most of these tiny houses on wheels are full-time homes, but not all—Jon, for example, has created a corrugated-tin retro-retreat in one corner of Sally's garden.

I would have loved to include a traveling storyteller's theater van in this chapter, too, but they were traveling at the time we were photographing!

Sally is an artist living in Suffolk and has a striking tiny house with a studio. Sally's tiny house was the result of many things, including being lucky enough to meet Jon Everitt. Jon is an artist of sheds and tiny houses, and has designed and built others both locally and in London. Jon built Sally's tiny house and converted an old garage in the garden into a studio.

On visiting Sally's main house, you see a stork's nest sculpture—complete with stork—on a post and a dragon posing by the drive. Sally paints two or three times a week and "has no excuse not to." Since the end of her last exhibition, there are still some paintings of striking textured trees and drawings of animals such as a camel and hippo to be seen.

Across the garden, with its South American- and Japanese-themed areas, is the tiny house. Sally asked Jon to build her new retreat in a once neglected corner of the garden with high hedges and a eucalyptus tree, which had been a "bit of a jungle." Jon had had his eye on this place to build "his dream house," which would also be a demonstration project.

When we met, Sally had had a busy summer with her art and exhibitions, including one in the converted studio, and Jon had been working in London on other commissioned sheds. As with his tiny house on wheels in Sweffling, in

LEFT Sally's friend, Jon, built a tiny home on wheels with a corrugated iron fascia. The large patio pots add contrasts of material and scale.

Suffolk, which he built on a glamping site, virtually all the materials are recycled and he finds creative solutions to using them. It is timber-framed with Critall® metal windows. There will be a wood-burning stove and ideas for the bathroom are yet to come.

When we arrived, they'd only just finished work on the tiny house—in fact, it had only been completed the day before. They had yet to sleep in the house, but had enjoyed a candlelit dinner there. Sally and Jon are both longing to start enjoying the space as a retreat, to read and write. As Sally says, "It fulfilled something for him and something for me."

The porch has a decorative scroll—one of Jon's findings—which is painted turquoise and there purely as a piece of ornamentation. The exterior is clad in corrugated tin, which looks striking against the deep green of the hedge. They think it "looks like an American chapel." The interior is full of collected items that are placed with care and yet with an appearance of relaxed juxtaposition, which is an art in itself, creating both beauty and balance. Jon sometimes combines materials that you might not expect to work together and he loves certain eras, having a knack of matching up materials and objects to create the feeling he wants.

The kitchen cabinets look to be from the mid-20th century and there's a 1950s breadbin and milk churn. On the shelves above sit a collection of old Bisto and OXO packaging, cans, and old books. A picture of a chicken hangs on the wall and a clock ticks in the background. An arrow points the way to a wooden ladder that leads up to the loft space. A tabletop gas stove and some old scales complete the tiny kitchen.

Beyond the kitchen is an eating space with a round metal table, a bench against a wall under the window, and some chairs. In the center of the table, there's a candleholder of dancing women. One of Sally's paintings hangs on one wall, while on another there's an old print tray that Jon has filled with matchboxes and cigarette packets from bygone days. A tobacco sign states "Cool and Mellow" and, on a blackboard,

ABOVE In the tiny dining area, there is seating and soft furnishings made with retro fabrics. There's a lovely view of the garden through the windows, one of Jon's many finds that give this home so much character.

OPPOSITE The retro detailing and furnishings in the tiny house are either made from recycled materials or are favorite found objects that reflect a love of times gone by.

ABOVE A set of ladder stairs leads up to an exotic loft bedroom, with a striking tapestry and multi-colored cushions. There are crates for books and other necessities. On display are some old posters and also a vintage Gold Flake advertising board, which make the space both kitsch and interesting.

is written, "One life—Live it" to reflect their aim of living in the creative present.

The tiny house has given them a completely revised perspective on the garden, a new appreciation of life, and a different view. Sally has planted silver birch trees in the garden and also installed some huge terracotta pots, tin troughs, and smaller pots for planting. The tiny house sits on slabs, which extend beyond the footprint of the wheelbase to provide a pleasant patio area for tables and chairs and for enjoying the new view.

"Jon built it all. I'm doing the planting in the garden... It will be really special to be there with a book and plant runner beans."

RIGHT The eating area has some of Sally's artwork hanging on the walls, including her painting of a camel. Elsewhere in the garden is her studio, which is another of Jon's successful conversions.

Gosia's wagon is beautifully built on an old hay-wagon chassis. Gosia lives in a Suffolk village in a farmhouse that adjoins acres of water meadows running alongside a small river. The hay wagon was used on the farm many years ago, but had sat in a field for five or six years before Gosia's friend Jon suggested making it habitable.

At first it was more visible to the neighbors, who didn't like it obstructing "their" view. The wagon needed to be at the top of the water meadow because it would have started to sink if positioned any farther down, so they moved it up the hill.

Jon found an arched window, which became the inspiration for the build, and, as Gosia says, the whole design fell into place from there. The arched window is framed on the inside by a pretty painted garland of twining ivy leaves. The seating/eating area is situated beneath the arched window, overlooking the meadows, where Gosia enjoys watching out for visiting wildlife such as deer, barn owls, and buzzards. They have also heard the whistling of otters and seen stoats. Not only is their wagon a home, it's also a wildlife hide. As Gosia says, "It is easy to lose a day with a telescope."

The design of the wagon was based on a showman's wagon, with a bed with a bit of storage underneath, an eating space, a wood-burning stove, and somewhere to prepare food. Jon built the initial framework and then the panels and cladding were added in situ. The ceiling is tongue-and-groove and Gosia painted the plywood surface around the arched window.

The seating is hand-built to be similar to the German bench design in her farmhouse kitchen. The strong Bavarian, Polish, and Russian influences in the wagon are a result of Gosia's heritage and background—she is Polish and was brought up in Bavaria for much of her life. She also loves Russian painted spoons and has been given spoons and trays by those that know her. Working as a market holder for two days a week in the local Suffolk town, she has a wide circle of friends who know her tastes well.

At the other end of the wagon, there's a bed. This needed to be 6ft 4in (1.9m) long, so that her son could sleep there. The bed is in a very self-contained area, some of which is obscured from view behind the shelves in the kitchen area. The bed was also influenced by Gosia's

LEFT Gosia has created a beautiful dining space with wooden seating and a dining table covered with a bright tablecloth. The table sits beneath the arched window—another of Jon's finds—which Gosia has framed beautifully with a leafy stencil design.

OPPOSITE The wood-burning stove, situated next to a pretty, fabric-covered cupboard, provides both heat and somewhere to keep the welcoming pair of kettles on the boil for hot water and cups of tea or coffee.

eastern European background, having a red-and-blue striped bed cover made from a Polish material that was traditionally used for women's skirts. Each skirt design is unique to the village or area of Poland from which it comes and can be "read," telling others where a woman is from. The design of the material used for the bed cover is from Lowicz, in central Poland. The red striped tablecloth is also made from the Lowicz design and lends brightness and jolliness to the space.

There is no sense of restraint in this sociable wagon, which is Gosia's own private place to be, as children and friends have lived there at one time or other. This tiny home welcomes both Gosia and her visitors, who can live there as the need arises. There have been up to 11 people sitting around the table enjoying a get-together. The welcome goes on.

FAR LEFT Beyond the wood-burning stove and cupboard is a sleeping alcove, with another of Gosia's Polish fabrics used as a bedcover and a curtain. The curtain can be drawn across for privacy and coziness.

LEFT A small shelf provides room for a few favorite drinking glasses, as well as somewhere to hang three decorative kitchen spoons.

The outside of the wagon will eventually be clad in timber and then it will be just right. It is the realization of Gosia's dream and one that was paid for by her "coffee money"—she has a traveling van from which she sells coffee at festivals.

The wagon is the first place of her own she has ever had and, apart from being a part-time living space, it is where she hopes to write the story of her Polish family, and of her mother and aunts' wartime experiences.

"Not only is the wagon a home, but it's also a wildlife hide. We can hear the high-pitched whistling of otters and have also spotted stoats. It is easy to lose a day with a telescope."

ABOVE Emma stays in her home on wheels in summer, especially when her Boer goats are giving birth, so she can help them if necessary.

RIGHT The old horsebox lorry is now a permanent feature in the fields, where Emma and Andrew can sit outside and light a fire in the evenings.

Emma and her partner, **Andrew**, have an old horsebox lorry, in Suffolk, England, which they found on ebay. They could see that it had lots of potential and Emma considered it to be "perfect." Emma was local to the area, so they were able to find some land and get the horsebox back and onto it in just two weeks. They can't live on this land all year round and only stay there in the summer and when the goats are kidding. But there the horsebox is to stay. They call her "Queenie." She was last used as a horsebox with living accommodation. "The horsebox was drivable," Emma says, "until last year, but would be hard to move now." As Emma says, "I made Queenie; it's my baby—my she-den."

To get to the field where the horsebox is kept, we walked down a long unmade track through wonderful, gently rolling hills close to the sea and the River Deben; there is nearly always a sea breeze.

Emma keeps South African Boer goats and Anglo-Nubian goats on the land. She breeds the pedigree Boer goats as a business, originally importing sperm from Australia to ensure the breed remained true, although they now have enough of the pedigree herd not to have to go down this route any more. The male goats supply meat, which she sells at a local market. The Anglo-Nubians are kept for their milk. Emma says she is known as "The Mad Goat Lady." The Boer goats are all named after different types of cloud/weather: Breeze, Nimbus, Cyrus, Typhoon, and Simoom—an Arabian wind. When we visited, the youngest goat was a day and a half old and within two weeks 19 kids (including a set of quintuplets) had been born to nine mothers, which is very unusual.

On arriving, we turned a corner behind some spring green-tinged trees, went through a gate, and saw the horsebox at the bottom of a hill in a field of goats. Emma carried out all the renovation work on the horsebox herself, apart from a bit of heavy lifting. The work included making the furniture and building the kitchen area. She wanted to live in a luxurious, "Orient-Express" style and has found wonderful oil lamps, mirrors, cupboards, and fittings to create the feeling she imagined. As Emma says, "'Queenie' was always going to be red, gold, and dark brown to give a Victorian feel." She wants the space "to be interesting, with nice things."

Solar panels provide enough electricity to power LED light fittings in the original oil lamps. The horsebox lorry is insulated, keeping it warm and cozy in the winter, and there's also a "La Rustica" Nordiga wood-burning stove for heating water. Hot water also comes from a large kettle and a small French kettle, which sings when it is boiling to make the tea. The larger kettle provides water for a hand-pumped shower and "enough to wash your hair." The stove came from friends who have a glamping business nearby and were upgrading theirs. They are hoping to find a plumber to install a heat-exchange system, which will make getting hot water much more efficient. The composting toilet, which was also found on ebay, is simple but adds a touch of glamour, as the bowl is gold and glittery!

LEFT Emma has created a luxurious interior that meets her needs for style and comfort. The old stove provides both warmth and plenty of room for cooking.

BELOW In the kitchen area, the units are all made by hand from dark wood. There are colorful recycled tiles above a large butler's sink.

Emma has created a luxurious raised bed under a stained-glass window at one end of the horsebox. The alcove for the bed is given privacy with a lace panel and curtains, and offers a fabulous view of the landscape and the goats when the window is open. There is plenty of storage beneath the bed and also some more hidden storage behind the reclaimed pub sign above the stove.

The lack of electronic entertainment, such as TVs, is no loss. Emma and Andrew talk more, read, and play cards. As Emma comments, "We are very good at small-space living and there is no fighting. It is like watching a dance." Sometimes they make a fire outside in the fire pit. Being in nature is important to them, as is being near to the goats that are such an important part of their lives. The most affectionate goats will sit with Emma for hours. Everything revolves around the goats.

The only noise to be heard is that of the wildlife and the "pop of the fire." They see stoats and roe deer and many birds. Emma calls the surrounding land "the place of birds" and adds, "The crows own it." There are also birds throughout the interior decoration, including on the splash-back tiles above the sink, on the cupboard handles, and in the bird mural on the plum-colored wall behind the stove.

Next to "Queenie" is another wagon called "Bertie," which Emma believes might have been a traveling salesman or showman's wagon. Emma says, "Poor Bertie needs some love." He is their next project.

ABOVE Emma's luxurious raised bed has a pretty lace panel and white drapes (curtains), which give a romantic feel to the space. There is useful storage below the bed. The view from the window enables Emma to keep an eye out for the goats and listen to nature's sounds, which she loves.

Dee is a painter who lives with her partner, **Richard**, on a farm in Suffolk, England. She works from her sofa in the main living area of this old showman's wagon. Dee's brushes sit on the windowsill behind her and many of her colorful paintings hang on the walls or lean against furniture in this creative home. As an artist, Dee has many followers and collectors, and also produces cards of people and places for those who are unable to afford her paintings.

Dee and Richard have lived on the farm for about two years after a period of moving around. They found that "in the real world, paying rent is not easy." They were very lucky because the farm belongs to Richard's father and they have been able to make their home there. They started off in the other rust-streaked caravan, which is now used for storage and somewhere to keep materials, as well as a cat haven. Dee says, "I am a bit of a hoarder." Although she could be a minimalist, the old caravan has become somewhere for her to hide

her belongings. As she explains, "I find it difficult to get rid of stuff." This is particularly true of things that once belonged to her grandmother. Dee elaborates, "The fact that they were hers is enough."

The wagon used to be owned by an ex-showman. It was in a poor condition when they found it and so they were able to buy it for £600 (US$ 780). Richard believes it to be a Sipson's fairground showman's wagon, possibly from the 1950s or '60s. It has a steel chassis, wooden frame, and aluminum cladding.

Everything had to come down so that they could put insulation in the roof. There was brown Formica cladding everywhere inside, but there is now only a diamond feature remaining on the sitting room ceiling, a "Tudoresque" detail they wanted to keep.

Dee and Richard altered the wagon to suit their needs and the kitchen is now where the sitting room used to be. There were three spaces, all with doors dividing them. They took these down and made the bedroom larger, putting in a new plywood wall with an open entrance from the kitchen, which is now only closed

BELOW The paintings in the bedroom are complemented by the bright bedding and the string of fairy lights, giving this artistic sanctuary a romantic feeling.

"It is difficult to be succinct in describing how and why I became an artist, or who has inspired and influenced me, because I have been producing and studying art and art history since I was three."

from view by a simple fabric hanging. Indeed, their evident love of color, fabrics, materials, and textures reflects the selection of colorful paintings on the walls. These are not only Dee's works of art, but also those of artist friends.

There are chickens wandering and scratching about outside, and cockerels sleep in the hedges, ensuring an early wakeup call—"they cackle before they get up and start crowing." Perhaps this is an early call to start painting, too? Dee tries to have set times for painting; daytime is not her favorite and she finds that she is most creative late in the day or at night when there are fewer distractions.

The living space has been expanded, as Richard built a cover for the wagon that extends over an outside area where there is room for a table and chairs, a refrigerator, and some shelving, and also somewhere to keep the bicycle. The floor is laid with recycled slabs and there are plans to enclose the extension fully. Richard builds as his ideas materialize. As he says, "It is a work-in-progress." The structure is supported by telegraph poles. This created another "room" that they can use in the summer and in milder winters.

Richard also has his own workshop for "all sorts of activity" where he can make and mend things, including bikes and guitars. Dee describes him as a "free spirit."

They love life on the farm, the farm buildings, and the natural decay. Indeed, Dee wants to explore making art about the environment in which they live. In the meantime, her quirky representations of old-fashioned-looking women and landscape views of the sea and countryside continue to charm and gain admirers. Dee started exhibiting locally in Bungay and now exhibits in Southwold and beyond.

Dee explains her life as an artist thus: "What could be more alluring than the clean sheet of paper, the array of drawing materials, the smell of the artist's studio, the feel of applying paint, the overwhelming wonder of paintings that exist, and the struggle of trying to achieve a satisfactory piece of art? When I was at art school, I was

anxious about having my own style and asked my tutor how to set about creating one. He said that I did actually have one already, even if I couldn't see it, and that the only way to achieve this was to continuously work and a distinctive one would emerge. I took his advice. And it has developed."

On living in this creative and artistic home, Dee says that she loves to have her precious things around her and also the security, freedom, and independence that this way of life makes possible.

ABOVE Dee's sitting room also acts as a studio space, where paintbrushes and other painting equipment nestle between decorative pieces.

RIGHT When Dee and Richard stripped out the old brown ceiling to put in some insulation, they wanted to retain the diamond pattern on the ceiling, which lends a "Tudoresque" feel to the living room.

OPPOSITE In the old, rust-stained caravan, which now acts as a storage room and closet, is Dee and Richard's cat's favorite sleeping spot—curled up tight in a basket.

Sitting in a wooded garden, in England's Norfolk, is a traveler's wagon. Belonging to **Bill and Janine**, its dark green sides are being renovated and will be painted once they've been mended and filled. The wagon was originally cream in color, but may have been black with religious messages painted on the side. Indeed, old photographs show similar dark wagons with white-painted messages such as, "The Only Way," "Give up Sin—Surrender to God—Where will you spend eternity?," and, more damningly, "The Wages of Sin is Death." Wagons such as these were commissioned by religious groups like The Salvation Army, the Quakers, and other non-conformist denominations.

In their heyday, in the 19th century, missionaries used preacher's wagons to roam from village to village in the summer, visiting festivals and markets to preach temperance and bring the locals to their own brand of God. Sometimes the missionaries would be in competition with each other at these events, which must have been quite a sight. Bill and Janine's wagon probably had one horse and, perhaps, a servant horseman who would sleep under the wagon. There are two iron steps on one side of the platform—this would have served as the preacher's pulpit, from where he could expound his sermons to the crowds.

The preacher's wagon used to belong to Bill's mother, who found it in a nearby village, and it was renovated over many years. The key to keeping the main structure safe was a good roof. Nevertheless, as Bill explains, as long as the metal work is sound, then these old wagons can be renovated. They just need a good skeleton. The front of the wagon had rotted away, but the main framework and old photographs enabled Bill to work out how to rebuild it.

When Bill inherited the wagon, he began renovating it in a way that would have met with his mother's approval. He concentrated initially on the interior of the wagon, so that he, Janine, and their family could live in it as soon as possible. After making the tin roof sound, the interior walls were repaired with tongue-and-groove paneling over new insulation. The insulation and a "barge-style" stove keep the wagon warm all year round. Originally, there may have been a pot-bellied stove. When the fire is lit, Bill says, the wagon comes to life. Light pours in through the windows in the raised mollicroft roof.

OPPOSITE This delightful preacher's wagon once traveled from fair to fair to spread the word and the virtues of temperance from the veranda, often in competition with other preachers equally determined that the masses should hear their particular message.

BELOW The name of the manufacturers of the wagon—the Bristol Wagon and Carriage Works Limited— is on the old wagon wheel.

ABOVE A wood-burning stove is set into a recess in the white cupboards to provide heat for the little wagon when there is a chill in the air.

LEFT The interior has been made to feel more spacious with white walls and pale green trims. The cupboards are all original. One of the cupboard doors drops down to provide a surface.

"When you are young, you guzzle the first part of the bottle but, as you reach the bottom, the whiskey becomes more precious and is supped with more care and appreciation.'"

BELOW The bed has a
pretty quilted cover, which
used to belong to Bill's
grandmother. It is in keeping
with the pastels that are
used throughout the rest of
the interior. The bed sits high
above the floor and provides
storage underneath. The two
chairs add a bright contrast
with their colorful throws.

Where possible, they try to furnish and decorate the wagon in a way
that wouldn't have seemed out of place in the 19th and early 20th
centuries. The windows may have had shutters, but are now waiting for
Janine to make curtains to transform the interior into a more feminine
space. When Bill and Janine have decided on the new color for the
exterior, this utilitarian wagon will be transformed into a lovely place to
stay. Bill muses that there is something to be said for taking a more
reflective view of life and not wasting time. An appreciation of good
craftsmanship has also come to him as a result of his renovation work.
The Preacher's Wagon will outlive him, as it will all of us. As Bill says,
"businesses and emails will disappear and mean very little."

ABOVE An al fresco eating area is used when friends come to visit.

OPPOSITE Alexis and Brian's home on wheels is clad in green aluminum and natural cedar sidings, which help it blend into its surroundings.

Alexis and Brian have a tiny home in a small clearing which is reached by a track through forested land, near Seattle, in the state of Washington, USA. The views of Mount Rainier are not to be had from there—rather they enjoy a more intimate relationship with nature and enjoy looking at a mountain view in a painting on the wall. They love being surrounded by nature and wildlife, and sometimes spot barn owls and spotted owls, which "liked to scare Brian" in the early days. Occasionally, they hear the call of barred owls and screech owls.

When Alexis and Brian decided to "live tiny," they found that it was not a straightforward path. After investigating other tiny house builders, they found Tina from Backcountry Tiny Homes. Tina helped with their "loose design," drawing on their combined research. They were able to "save a ton of money" by doing as much as possible themselves.

Alexis and Brian's previous lives involved going down "the rabbit hole" each day, with long commutes to jobs that weren't satisfying,

"If we are lucky, we spot barn and spotted owls, and if we're very lucky, we can hear barred owls' amazing calls and the eerie sound of the screech owl."

no money, and no free time. They now have local jobs, with reduced commuting times, making time at home with their dog more satisfying and enjoyable.

At first Brian struggled with the idea of being debt-free, which goes against so much of the debt-slavery culture we are used to. It has taken them 10 years to achieve their debt-free goal, with most of this being accomplished in the first five years.

Brian put up a whole side of the house and they both fell in love with every bit of the build. They even gave the planks names! The outside of

"I like to be close to Alexis all the time... we still like each other! We like to throw our clothes up and down the stairs. I can sit everywhere and talk about whatever!"

ABOVE The kitchen area feels spacious and well-designed, with woodblock countertops and a white sink under a row of windows. These give a peaceful view of the forest.

OPPOSITE Brian and Alexis have created a smart interior that cleverly uses every available space for storage and to provide comfort. The light walls contrast with the wood of the detailing and the ceiling, and there is also an open-plan loft bedroom.

the building is clad with hardy materials, including cedar and dark green
aluminum sidings. Using different materials creates visual contrast, and
both these materials are also hardwearing and weatherproof. Their
water comes from a well and electricity is generated using solar panels.
They have created an eating area outside for themselves and friends.

Inside they needed to be practical and bring in as much light as
possible, due to the forest location. Eighteen windows let in the soft
forest light. Maximizing the height of the interior has created a feeling
of space and comfort in this romantic retreat.

ABOVE One bedroom area
leads to the other, with a
cat walkway running over
the seating and desk areas
below. Underneath the far
loft is a sliding door to the
bathroom, which incorporates
a ladder for climbing to bed.

There are two sleeping lofts and Tina, who helped with the build, designed an ingenious sliding door to the bathroom, which also acts as a convenient ladder that can be climbed to reach the little guest loft. The other loft, which is their bedroom, is located up the steps opposite. It is a pretty, light-filled room with a dash of bright color from a bedthrow and strings of fairy lights around the ceiling.

The walls are white shiplap and the ceilings are clad with a beautiful pine: Beetle Kill Pine, in which the beetles' destruction trails leave a striated pattern. They were able to source this recycled wood and other materials. As they say, "We feel good about this."

There is a cat-feeding ledge and the cat has a home under the stairs. They tucked a desk into an alcove—also lined with Beetle Kill Pine—next to the sofa. Under the sofa, there's a pull-out table for coffee, relaxing, and just putting up their feet.

When we visited, Alexis and Brian had just moved in a month ago and only managed to get hot water in the past week. There was also a rickety stair arrangement to the front door, while they wait for a new one to be put in. So, it is all new and very exciting... they love their "Sweet Reveal." As Brian quips, "The most important thing is that we can clean it in an hour." They are having fun.

RIGHT Beyond the living area and the work desk is the wood-lined bathroom, which is cleverly designed with a dark wood sliding door.

"It is a natural human instinct to build shelter... but it need not fall apart."

Hannah built her tiny house on wheels in her parents' yard, in Seattle, USA. She has made building tiny houses into a business, and also teaches about and demonstrates tiny-house living. Her business is called Pocket Mansions, which she runs from her parents' house. Hannah is building another tiny house in Dakota.

Hannah thinks that the huge interest in tiny houses, particularly in Seattle, is because people see them as the only way to have a home in "the fifth most expensive city in the world." She had the option of living with her parents, sharing, looking into co-housing, or leaving Seattle, but none of these would have suited her. Although she thought that it would prove impossible, she needed the freedom and privacy of living in her own home. Hannah's father had built the family home where she was born, so house building was in her blood. It was only when she saw tiny houses online that the possibility of building her own tiny abode became apparent.

When Hannah decided to construct her own tiny home, some people asked, "Are you really going to build your own house?" She believes that this question would not have been asked of a man. However, she worked with a carpenter "who knew how to build... it was a fun little vacation for him." She did her research and designed her tiny home with his help. She comments, "If you can plan and manage a budget, it is possible." She believes many people like the idea of building their own home, but stresses that you must have the time and energy to get to the end of the project, which can be problematic for some. Hannah admits to being a perfectionist and had to work out what sacrifices she was willing to make so that she could have her perfect home—she wanted all the comforts, only on a smaller scale. Eventually, her tiny house was created on what was once her father's pumpkin patch and finished in 2015.

When teaching, Hannah asks people to do a reality check to help them work out if building their own home might be an unrealistic dream. She says, "I have heard some really horrible stories." She has created a myth-buster page online to help people decide if it really is for them. She is practical about building codes and size requirements, which vary from state to state. The tiny home movement is beginning to gain traction with the authorities and, in Idaho, tiny houses have been included in the Idaho Building Safety rules. If the tiny house is constructed according to the building standards of NOAH (National Organization of Alternative Housing), there is a possibility of getting insurance. Sometimes, Hannah says, "It can feel bleak... meeting with officials and lobbying sometimes very resistant officials." She thinks that change will come state by state. She jokes that her tiny home is "legally a boat!"

Hannah's house is timber-framed with cedar shingle cladding. The framework is made from Douglas fir, the flooring from hardwearing bamboo, and the ceiling cladding from knotted cedar. The roof is made of copper-colored steel. Hannah loves the color of it so much she treated herself to a hammered copper sink with matching-colored tile trim detailing in the kitchen and a freestanding copper basin in the bathroom. Decorative copper pitchers (jugs) hang from pegs in the kitchen and she also has a kettle made from the same metal. The countertops are made from Corian® embedded with copper flakes.

BELOW The seating area, next to the entrance, is adaptable, with a fold-out table and pretty seats, which are covered with a fabric that was once Hannah's mother's. There are matching curtains at the windows.

Downstairs there's a seating area that converts into an extra bed. Hannah's mother made the seat covers and matching curtains in a "mid-20th-century print." A folding table for meals is built into the seating area. There is a "faux" fireplace with a mantelpiece, where she can imagine sitting by a real fire by lighting candles in the grate.

On high shelves downstairs is her collection of Cupcake Dolls—"just the right size for a tiny house." She also has her grandfather's record player and some of his records, while upstairs hang pictures of her great grandmother and great grandfather.

The stairs needed to be "proper" for Hannah and she has incorporated drawers and shelving underneath for storage. The washer-dryer and microwave are also under the stairs. These lead up to her bedroom, which is partly screened from view by a shelf of favorite

BELOW The copper kettle complements the sink and tesserae behind the countertop, showing how luxurious elements can make the difference to a tiny space.

ABOVE Another copper sink, with an old-fashioned faucet (tap), stands on top of the Oriental-style cabinet in the little bathroom at the back of Hannah's tiny home.

LEFT The stairs to the bedroom loft cleverly incorporate the washer-dryer and microwave, and there is an ingenious laundry shute from the loft so Hannah can avoid carrying washing downstairs. The bookshelf is filled with Hannah's favorite cookery books.

cookery books from when she used to be a pastry chef, and children's books from her childhood. She has plenty of hanging space and shelves by the bed, and there is a nifty laundry shute down which Hannah can send her laundry into a basket in the utility cupboard behind the stairs.

In the bathroom the vanity cupboard is cleverly set into the next-door shed. An Oriental-style cupboard supports the lovely copper basin with its old-fashioned faucet (tap). The quality of Hannah's design and her attention to detail are evident throughout the tiny house.

Hannah believes, "Small is Beautiful"—quoting from E. F. Schumacher's book *Small Is Beautiful: A Study of Economics As If People Mattered*, which he wrote in 1993. However, she doesn't find that the tiny house feels small. The height created by the two levels for the roof give an impression of spaciousness. She believes it is possible to draw the eye with the clever placement of objects.

Mari has found an idyllic and beautiful spot in which to live, with a wonderful view of the magnificent, snow-topped Mount Rainier, on a rural farm in south-east King County, in the state of Washington, USA. The farm belongs to Cal and Rebecca, and Mari, as well as a young couple, Chris and Tatiana (see pages 118–19), have been made very welcome there. Cal and Rebecca's warmth and hospitality means the community and the whole place feel very welcoming. As Cal says, "We all get along really well." They have a sense of community and mutual support, in addition to the privacy they want

Mari's unique home was carefully designed to her precise specifications, which included being both beautiful and practical to meet her physical needs (Mari uses a walking frame). Mari sold her original house in 2016, before moving into her tiny rural home and starting her new life there. She loves the design, which ended up exactly how she imagined it would.

For a year Mari gave stuff away to friends and share-house schemes for homeless people, finding the process of paring down easy. She also had a stall at a rummage sale, although she found it strange to be selling rather than buying stuff.

ABOVE Mari lives in a colorful tiny home on wheels on a farm with fabulous views of Mount Rainier.

"Everything is important to me and the only freestanding furniture is on the deck, which a friend, Buddy, built. He was so inspired by my tiny house that he hopes to buy land in Idaho and follow the same dream."

As Mari explains, "It was a problem to find somewhere to put my tiny home." So she put a request on Facebook and Rebecca responded. Although Mari was "not quite ready," they met. Mari jokes, "I carried out a background check on myself and the meeting went really well!" After a vacation with her daughter, Mari agreed to Rebecca's offer of a place to put her tiny house. It all "sort of happened" from there and she moved that September. Electricity and water could be obtained via Cal and Rebecca's farmhouse, and so Mari began her new life. She put straw bales around the base of the house, which cut out drafts and provide a raised area for growing salad crops inside the bales.

The patio has both steps and a ramp, and is also a wonderful place to relax and take in the spectacular view. A table and chairs are shaded by a jolly umbrella and also blue window awnings, while bright flowerpots bring further color to the exterior. The final touch of zing comes from the turquoise-painted edges of the deck and ramp.

Inside, Mari's custom-made bed is downstairs in an area with a room divider, behind which she keeps her walking frame. There's also a shelf around the top of the wall that acts as a cat highway for her cats, Spike and Moses. Staggered steps on the bedroom wall lead up to the shelf, where the cats like to sleep. There is even a drawer under the seat just for the cats' food, with a little cat-sized door going into it— otherwise, given the chance, her dog, Baba, would eat all their food. The cats' needs are truly met.

The main part of Mari's tiny home features the kitchen and seating area. A threefold table, which is stored against the dividing wall, is made of natural oak and the cracks filled with crushed turquoise glass and resin, adding to this mini work of art and craft. Unpretentiously Mari says, "A couch is a couch," but this is also a storage and cat-feeding station. Mari loves rabbits and so rabbit wallpaper left over from her last house was used to face the kitchen cabinets. The cabinets and all the carpentry were handmade by the designer at exactly the right

BELOW The clever design of Mari's home makes it work for her particular needs. The designer incorporated pieces of loved furniture into the shelving and storage units.

ABOVE The needs of the dog and cats have not been ignored in the clever design; these staggered steps for the cats lead up to a cat walkway.

OPPOSITE Mari's home is comfortable, with inviting seating and a fold-down table for meals. The table can be tucked away when it's not in use, but is also a sculptural piece in its own right.

height for Mari. The pull-out pantries and shelves store her food mixer, food, and kitchen utensils, and a microwave/convection cooker, which saves on space, as well as being practical.

The surfaces of the countertops and the floor are Marmoleum, which is extremely hardwearing and easy to keep clean. Mari explains that any dents can be mended by grinding down some spare Marmoleum and mixing it with glue to make a filler.

The bathroom has an unusual feature in the shape of a cupboard door to the outside of the house, so that Mari can put the garbage directly into containers.

Memories are captured in the interior design, with spindles from her mother's old table and drawers from an old coffee table being used to create some shelving above the sink.

The designer of Mari's tiny home also created stairs leading up to a loft where guests can stay. Roof lights and windows mean natural light floods into this area. She is going to ask her cousin to make a stained-glass window to add a further decorative feature to her home.

Outside the tiny house, two young goats run free, causing much amusement as they break into a gallop while playing with Mari's young neighbors. As Mari comments, "A tiny house—a great mountain."

"The cats have some staggered steps on the bedroom wall that lead up to the shelf. They sleep on the shelf and enjoy looking at me in my room."

Mark and Kara met and got married on a blueberry farm, where they were blueberry picking 13 years ago. The farm was near Mount Si, a mountain on the western margin of the Cascade Mountain Range that looms above the coastal plains around Puget Sound. This is an inlet of the Pacific Ocean and part of the Salish Sea. They had been renting and were locked into a year's lease. They say, "We were chasing our tails and having difficulty keeping up with rent." Mark and Kara's vision and dream of living on a farm brewed for five years.

ABOVE At one end of the tiny home a garden window is set into the kitchen wall so Mark and Kara can grow herbs and keep an eye on the chicken run and passing wildlife.

BELOW Mark and Kara's black home, with its blue-green door and white window surrounds, stands out dramatically in farmland with a view of Mount Si.

Kara's mother had been watching lots of tiny house shows on television and said to them, "You could do that." It was the discovery of tiny houses and being able to live a more frugal life on the land that began their journey. The seed was planted. They jumped at the chance, saying, "Let's do that!" Something had to change, but where were they going to put their new home? They trusted that this question would be answered in time and researched tiny houses, "opening up a Pandora's Box" as they looked at builders, styles, and materials. They asked questions, such as "What do we really need?", "How can we have freedom and financial security?", and "How can being a consumer reflect our self worth?".

The opportunity arose through a chance conversation in the Co-op where Kara was working. This led to a meeting with Alison, who was building a tiny house, and from there, to Sharon Read, the founder of Seattle Tiny Homes. Sharon and Alison helped them custom-design their new home. The design was "ambiguous" to allow for any future changes, such as having a family. They decided on a 28-ft (8.5-m) custom-built trailer and visited other tiny homes until Sharon came up with a CAD (Computer Aided Design) they liked. There were emails, calls, and edits, as questions came up they hadn't even thought of.

Their tiny house sits on Alison's land, with a magnificent view of Mount Si. Kara and Mark are both nature-lovers, so this is the ideal location for them. The land they ended up on was reasonably flat; they were offered a Mini Farm Lease and began clearing. In the first year, they cleared 300 square feet (28 square meters) and by the end of the second year 1,200 square feet (111 square meters) had been cleared.

The build took 10 months from start to finish. Kara says, "It was like having a baby!" The day their tiny home turned up was an "Oh my God!" moment. Maneuvering their

"On the day we moved in, I saw fifteen rainbows... it was an Easter miracle. We were jazzed about it!"

BELOW Each step of the staircase to the loft also provides storage with shelves and a microwave above a useful cupboard. Beyond is the well-designed kitchen so Mark and Kara can prepare and cook, which they love.

LEFT The ceiling height had to accommodate a full-sized refrigerator. Every detail of the kitchen, including the walnut countertops, was carefully thought out by this food-oriented couple.

BELOW The interior is lined with pine tongue-and-groove paneling, with a sliding door that has an attached ladder to give access to the "hangout" loft. Behind the door is the bathroom, with another of the couple's requirements— a full-sized bathtub.

tiny home into position was an adventure in itself, because it was pouring with rain and they had to get it over the gravel road and onto the slabs.

When we met, they had only been living in their tiny house for four weeks. Every detail has been considered, including the design of the pull-down faucets (taps) in the kitchen. The countertops are made from oiled walnut butcher's blocks. The couple are all about food—growing it, talking about it, and cooking it. Mark wanted a full-sized refrigerator, which determined the loft height. They have pull-out shelves under the stairs to the loft for storage and appliances. The kitchen takes up most of the floor space.

The interior is lined with pine tongue-and-groove paneling and the windowsills are made from stained hemlock. The window above the sink is a "conservatory or garden window" for growing herbs and salads. It also gives a great view of the land. The walls are whitewashed to enhance the wood grain. Decoration is kept to a minimum, which gives their tiny house a peaceful and uncluttered style. Only a pretty mirror hangs on the wall and simple contemporary lighting adds a sculptural quality.

With the kitchen being the star of their tiny home, there is not much room for any other furniture, but there is a pretty yellow chair and a small octagonal table. The stairs provide

additional seating space. Double glass doors let in the light and open out to the wonderful view. They are painted blue-green, so giving the space a dash of color. Above the door is an arrow pointing toward Mount Si. Outside, the frame of the door looks vivid against the black exterior walls.

There is a sliding barn door with a ladder built onto it for ascending to the "hangout" loft. Behind the door, there's a simple bathroom with a full-size bath—one of their requirements—and subway tiled walls. Their own bedroom loft has a large bed with a colorful rug and views of the surrounding land and mountain.

It turned out that Alison was into permaculture and so Mark and Kara's other dream of having land and farming started to become a reality. They too have an interest in Permaculture Design, which works with nature and not against it. Now they have chickens, which they move about using a movable chicken tractor, and a rooster called "Johnny Cash." They have begun a permaculture spiral, which is expanding as they clear and plant. They have garlic and strawberries so far. Their priority is the animals at the moment. The next project is to build a duck tractor. Kara says, "We need to build electric fences to keep out the coyotes, elk, deer, and foxes." They have seen an elk on the land every night since they have been there.

They are still planning to get solar panels to provide power but, for now, they are hooked up to Alison's house.

Mark and Kara's future in their perfect tiny house on the land with the view is beginning a very exciting phase of their lives.

ABOVE The loft bedroom is lined with pine and has wonderful views of the countryside, the farm, and Mount Si from the double bed. The colorful throw and pillows on the bed provide a nice contrast with the wood.

Carmen and Tom spent three years designing their tiny home, which is now nestled in the foothills of the Cascade Mountains in the state of Washington, USA. Carmen is a registered nurse who used to work in insurance appeals. Tom is an accountant who does the accounts for the owner of the land where they now live. As they say, "We didn't want to have to work for the rest of our lives." Their tiny house was custom-built by Tiny Idahomes in Idaho. It was a challenge to build to meet Carmen and Tom's needs and there was much to-ing and fro-ing to get it right. It was "delivered to Oregon, went back to North Idaho, and then was brought to our spot." They went on to say, "We are hoping not to move a ton more."

Carmen and Tom used to live in a huge house and when they moved they had to get rid of a lot of stuff, including their books. But Carmen feels that their tiny house is not spartan in any way and adds that there is beauty in what is necessary. Carmen says, "Tom is a borderline hoarder, so we decided what we wanted to keep." They were able to get rid of stuff relatively easily.

ABOVE Carmen and Tom's tiny home nestles in the foothills of the Cascade Mountains. They found a spot, surrounded by agricultural clutter, behind an agricultural factory workshop, which contrasts strikingly with the beautiful forest and hills around them.

OPPOSITE Carmen didn't stint on design and loves the "French storybook style." She limited her choice of colors to grays, teal, and pinks, with purple highlights, and opted for a hardwearing, faux-wood floor treatment.

Carmen and Tom live with their daughter, Lauren, in their tiny home behind a large "industrial" workshop. You would imagine they'd have preferred to live on the green slopes away from the scrap metal and old tires, but they like being hidden away. Though they add, "We didn't like the junk at first." However, they have great views of the trees from the back of their tiny home. It is an extraordinary tiny house, juxtaposed as it is against agricultural industry and the surrounding forest. Outside the tiny house is painted white, but with black outlines to the panels and bright turquoise detailing around the windows.

Carmen designed everything for the interior, from the colors and general design to the choice of accessories. She even searched for the right faucets (taps) on the Internet and the Ralph Lauren Metallic Blue paint for the doors. This tiny house has considered and beautiful accessories with the bathroom winning first prize. The kitchen and bathroom were given paramount importance in terms of comfort and design. Indeed, the bathroom has a wonderful, deep blue washbasin. It is set on a beautiful translucent Corian shelf made from leftovers, which incorporates pale turquoise LED lights. Above the basin is an ornate carved mirror from the 17th or 18th century that Carmen painted silver herself. She wanted a "French storybook look" and so there is

ABOVE The bathroom is Carmen's pride and joy, with its bespoke blue washbasin. For Carmen, it is the beautiful focus of their home.

TOP This tall family designed everything, including the height of the countertops, to suit them, so they can feel comfortable in their kitchen.

also a pink chandelier. When the room is lit up at night, this creates a magical glow and they often leave the bathroom door open so that they can enjoy this unusual focus point. In the bathroom area, there's a useful floor-to-ceiling storage unit of shiny, white drawers—some for Tom, some for Carmen, and some for Lauren. There are bathroom drawers, cleaning drawers, hat and scarf drawers, and more.

Carmen and Tom have accessible stairs to their relaxing loft bedroom. Their bed is a "split Queen" that can be moved to zero gravity, as it works like a recliner. The space is very comfortable, which means Carmen can work in the bedroom. As she says, "I love to lie in bed listening to the rain and the frogs and all the other sounds of nature"—even those that they can't identify. "There are deer and rabbits, snakes and owls."

Lauren's room, situated above the porch, has her keyboard, long shelves for her belongings, and several thousand well-organized DVDs. "We are all movie buffs!"

They all love the wild location of their home, enjoying nature and going hiking; next year Carmen and Lauren plan to walk the Pacific Crest Trail. "We designed a house that's us. It doesn't feel tiny and has a feeling of being bigger inside than it appears from the outside." It makes Carmen happy and Lauren adds, "Me too!"

BELOW The contemporary wood-burning stove is a focal point of Carmen and Tom's living space. The tiny home already has plumbing systems in place, ready for when they install solar panels.

RIGHT The limited seating in the dining area requires that the stairs to the loft also provide somewhere for Carmen and Tom to sit. Beyond the kitchen is a view of the detritus that comes from living in a factory yard.

Ryan and Daphne live in a rented house in Wenatchee in the foothills of the Cascade Mountains, in the state of Washington, USA. Their house on wheels is a work-in-progress in the yard of their rented home. Working out other living arrangements while they construct their mobile home pushes them on, but there is no compromise on the quality of the build. They both have jobs in Wenatchee, which restricts the time they have to spend on the new building. Ryan bought a Tumbleweed Tiny House plan, which formed the basis of the build. They simply adapted the plan from the beginning to meet their own needs.

The timber-framed building is insulated, but not finished inside. Daphne wanted a Dutch (stable) door that opened at the top, so Ryan made this happen. They would like a hexagonal or octagonal window in the loft and skylights. The eco-friendly roof, made from tile strips called Onduvilla®, has a 135mph (217kph) wind tolerance and a lifetime warranty, as well as being made from 60 percent recycled materials.

The stairs to the loft area will be designed to resemble a tree with branches and there will be feature shelves beneath. They plan to trim with natural split logs and give their home a rustic feel, while still retaining the comforts they need and making contemporary use of aluminum and stainless steel. The floor will be made of compressed bamboo, which is very hardwearing and beautiful. Ryan and Daphne find the whole process exciting, from the working out of loads and materials to the building calculations, and have been inspired by tiny houses and other housing solutions, including designs for earth and tire buildings in Texas.

Ryan and Daphne realize that there is more scope for finding a place for their mobile home on the east side of the Cascade Mountains, where there will be less potential pressure from neighbors concerned about the value of their properties. Tiny houses are not everyone's vision for enhancing a neighborhood, no matter how beautiful they may be. However, as Ryan says, "locals and passers-by are excited by it."

This way of living will meet their deeply felt desire to remain debt-free and not to live above their means. As long as they have wheels and a tow bar, they'll make it. Daphne adds, "Towing the home will be nerve-wrecking," but Ryan has built it to last. As she says, 'I'm not going to spend my time building our home to have it fall down." Their plans for the future are fully achievable and they only need to decide where to live in their mobile home—be this in Colorado or Georgia, where Daphne has family. Wherever they end up, there will be "puppies, tools, the tiny house—and a backyard."

OPPOSITE The build of this home started in a yard in Wenatchee on the far side of the Cascade Mountain Range. It will move when Ryan and Daphne find a new location for their home on wheels.

BELOW Cleverly, the couple moved the refrigerator and oven into the build before creating the doors. Everything else will be built in later, including steps to the loft with its branch-like roof struts.

Chris and Tatiana's tiny home is situated on the same idyllic farm as Mari's tiny house (see pages 104–107), south of Seattle, in the state of Washington, USA. They discovered their home through family and friends of Rebecca and Cal, the owners of the farm. In late 2014, the young couple had begun thinking about how they wanted to live and what they had to do to achieve their home. They began saving and had enough put aside to buy the trailer by the end of the following year. They bought their plans from Wishbone Tiny Homes, in North Carolina. They explain that they don't "use them as an ABC," but instead as a framework to help them construct their home and meet building codes.

Chris and Tatiana's home is only three-quarters finished. They began it in June 2016 but, with the pressure of employment, have found that progress is spasmodic. They work on their house at weekends. As Tatiana says, "It is pretty much a friends-and-family affair." Chris took four months off work, which enabled him to crack on and get the basics done. Enough has been completed for them to live there—they have somewhere to sit and a bed up in the loft.

The home looks pretty complete from the outside. They plan to use T1-11 cedar siding, a plywood material that has the right look, but is more economical than true cedar siding. They will also use some cedar shiplap. The windows have pine trims and the roof is metal. At present, the steps leading to the front door are a mish-mash of wood and pallets. Tatiana says, "Everything will happen in its own good time."

ABOVE Chris and Tatiana's home on wheels is situated on the same farm as Mari's tiny home (see pages 104–107), with the same gorgeous view of Mount Rainier. The mountain is covered with snow, even in the summer.

"We don't want to be tied down by money for the rest of our lives. We want to be free to explore with our three dogs and our cat."

Chris and Tatiana met when they were college students. Chris did a degree in marine biology in Olympia. Tatiana went to the "Hippy College of the Country"—The Evergreen State College, which is also in Olympia. They plan to use recycled materials wherever possible when building their new home. As they explain, "We made a choice not to be in debt any more after our school debt."

One evening Tatiana came home from work to find the tiny house set up for a romantic dinner with strings of fairy lights and candles. On the floor Chris had stenciled: "Will you marry me?" They are now building a new life together in this idyllic place, with wonderful neighbors and their whole future in front of them.

BELOW The exterior of Chris and Tatiana's home is nearly complete, with just a veranda and steps still to be built. The cladding will be T1-11 cedar siding with some additional natural cedar shiplap.

Chapter four
ECO HOMES

A great many of the tiny homes in other chapters of this book have some eco-credentials, and could perhaps be called eco homes. But the ones in this chapter have a range of eco-friendly features, from being off-grid to having a construction that is as energy efficient, and has as low an impact on the environment, as possible—which is important to the owners of these tiny homes.

Many of the featured eco homes, such as Devin's quirky treehouse north of Seattle, are built from locally sourced and recycled materials. Devin learnt as he went along, using the materials to build organically—for example, around the "found" windows.

The two whisky barrel houses at The Findhorn Foundation Village are a very unusual "recycle," which, amazingly enough, do not smell of whisky. Findhorn is a mecca for eco-builders and the lovely timber-framed and -clad row of houses in Centires Terrace was also built to be more affordable. One of these terraced houses belongs to Bryony and Liam, while next door is "The Honeypot," which was once hexagonal. Local materials, custom-made furniture, and bamboo flooring are all a part of this environmentally sensitive home.

Insulation is key to keeping heating costs down. Dürten's little wooden Findhorn roundhouse only needs a wood-burning stove to keep it warm, as it is so well insulated. And although Andy built under-floor heating in his strawbale house, in Somerset, the good insulation means he never needs to use it.

Some people choose to live off-grid completely, such as Dave in his shack, Marcus in his roundhouse, and Firefly and Johann in their yurt hidden in a field—no utility bills for them. Like Firefly and Johann's yurt and its extensions, John and Mary's caravan and yurt grew with the arrival of a little one and they found that innovative, natural, and organic solutions were the answer.

Devin's life, up until the building of the treehouse in his parents' forest north east of Seattle, was that of a traveler. Traveling is important to Devin because it empowers him to experience and appreciate what he calls "the full spectrum of being human." He had been traveling for a year and a half. He met Katie when he came home and decided not to head off again, but to settle down with Katie instead.

The decision not to live with his parents, or be tied down by a lease agreement, led to one of his "best moments... a romantic one as well." Devin decided that a treehouse would be the perfect residence for both of them, so he embarked on designing and building his own. He gained his carpentry skills through building and living in the treehouse. "I purchased tools from pawn shops and borrowed. As there was no electricity, my good friend and building partner, Jack, lent me his generator. I would regularly bribe my friends with beer for their help. The value of their help cannot be overstated."

Devin began work at the time of the economic collapse of 2008, which was tragic for those who lost their homes or were in the process of building, but meant that perfectly good materials were readily available. However, as Devin explains, "Not all the materials came with a sour note." A barn had collapsed a couple of years before the build and so the framing for the treehouse was made from good Douglas fir from the barn. The flooring and walls came from an old lumberjack's house that was no longer in use. Devin says, "The materials were given to me for free, as long as I took all of them." He explains that some of the materials were more than a century old. The decking and stairs were milled locally from a spruce tree that had recently fallen.

It was these materials, as well as a motley collection of windows Devin had acquired, that influenced the design of the treehouse. "If I had a window I wanted to include, I designed the wall around it." The multitude of windows and glass doors lets in a soft, green, dappled light. About 90 percent of the materials were free and/or recycled, and all in all probably cost about US $5,000 (£3,800).

Devin thought he was alone in the tree-house world in Washington, but, as his own treehouse construction began, he met Pete Nelson from

RIGHT Devin moved out of his "crooked" treehouse when he and Katie were expecting a child, leaving this build in the woods as a monument to his inventiveness.

the Nelson Treehouse and Supply company. He showed them his portfolio and began working for them as a treehouse carpenter. As well as experiencing the joy of building his own treehouse, he now enjoys building treehouses for others.

Devin's treehouse has a platform that's reached by stairs. Reflecting the triangular construction around the three trees, this platform has three rustic benches along each side. Then, going up, there is a sitting room where his guitar still hangs under the ladder to the sleeping loft high up in the cedar trees. The crookedness of the design, with all the different angles and views, is constantly surprising and engaging.

Devin recommends a treehouse for those who are interested in living there full-time and also committed to the "outdoorsy, pared-down lifestyle." He says treehouse life can be "a liberating, mindful, and

ABOVE Devin used found materials and created the build using what he could source or was given. Most of the recycled materials dictated the organic build, with Devin learning his skills as he went along.

joyful experience." However, he cautions that it can also be hard work, uncomfortable, and unsustainable, depending on the health of the host trees, climate patterns, life changes, and more. For example, as time wore on, Devin and Katie found the absence of plumbing presented a hurdle: without it, doing dishes and showering became a chore, as they had to lug gallons of water up to their arboreal home. But, if you thoroughly consider these factors, "so much about living in the treehouse was wonderful, from the closeness to nature to the simplicity of the lifestyle." He found that the joy of waking up in the trees never wore off.

There is electricity, so living in the trees includes light, media, a refrigerator, and a heater for cold days and nights—this is a rustic life away from others, yet also a connected one. The silence is only interrupted by the calls of birds echoing all around. Mesh at the windows keeps out the insect life that is less welcome.

"I had a constant appreciation of my environment while I was living there. There was a deep satisfaction in feeling as if I had earned the space I was occupying. There was no part of my surroundings that I was alienated from... I look back on my time there very fondly. I had spent two years building it and a little over

ABOVE The windows are all different, giving quirky and surprising views of the trees around which Devin designed the treehouse.

two years living in it. This was a pivotal time in my life. The intentions I had with regard to impressing Katie had worked. She also lived there with me for much of the time. We are now married and expecting our first-born. It has also given me my career. I was able to take that first build and steamroll it into my current profession, which is building treehouses. Living in such a small space, disconnected from the world, was a great way to spend a couple of years. I was able to read a lot, find patterns in the nature around me, and whittle my life down to its essentials... apart from a few luxuries."

LEFT The first flight of stairs wraps around the treehouse. Natural wood was used for the balustrades and handrails, which have LED lights.

Auriol was on a trip to South Africa when she met Eileen Caddy and her second husband Peter. Eileen and Peter were two of the original founders of the intentional community at The Findhorn Foundation (see page 34) at the Findhorn Ecovillage, near Inverness, in Scotland. The community that Eileen and Peter started in 1962, with their close friend Dorothy Maclean, was one of the first modern intentional communities. Auriol was very much inspired by Eileen, who was a spiritual teacher and New Age author.

Some years later, while Auriol was working and renting in Sussex, she had to vacate her home when the owner wanted it back. She had not wanted to leave and didn't want to be "kicked out again." The experience left her with a burning desire for a long-term solution. It was at this time that she heard about a whisky barrel house being built at The Findhorn Foundation. She raised the money and was able to work with the architect, Nicole Edmunds, who has a practice in Forres, near Findhorn. Nicole designed the building and her husband, who was a "brilliant carpenter," made the building into a "musical instrument." You can play music in any room in the barrel house and not know where it is coming from.

The accommodation in the barrel house is split over two floors, and there's also a half-basement room. The balcony terrace outside the kitchen on the first floor has steps leading down to a backyard on a gentle slope with pine trees behind.

The barrel is held together with gigantic copper bands and, because the walls slope slightly inward, birds perching on the large bolts means the windows need cleaning more often! Her Siamese cat is sunning herself on the windowsill when we visit.

The spare room in the slightly underground basement gives a feeling of being among the roots of the barrel house and a small, hobbit-like door opposite the room opens into a large underground cellar.

Auriol's Whisky Barrel House was the second one to be built at The Findhorn Foundation. It is situated next to Roger's (see pages 130–133)—his was the first barrel

OPPOSITE Auriol's house was the second of its kind to be built at The Findhorn Foundation. The ground floor is built from stone, with the "barrel" providing the second floor.

"The acoustics of the building are such that music being played in the downstairs spare room can be heard anywhere. You just don't know where the music is coming from."

BELOW A balcony on the upper floor leads to the gently sloping "natural" garden, with views of the pine trees that surround this unusual home.

house to be built. Auriol's is a bit bigger and sits in a pretty garden area with silver birches, heathers, and well-placed rocks and stones. A path leads up to an inviting flagstoned area outside the porch.

The walls of the first floor are built of stone, with the whisky barrel built above this to provide the second floor. A zinc cone roof tops it all off. The roundness and the use of materials produce a pleasing shape that sits comfortably in the Scottish landscape. To Auriol, the "materials matter" and they have complementary qualities.

BOTTOM The kitchen was custom-made to fit the walls by a carpenter who put together the cabinets and countertops like a big jigsaw.

BELOW Auriol's cat enjoys a sunny spot on a windowsill that has prime views of the birdlife outside.

Stuart, who is renowned in the Findhorn community for his stonework, made the foundations and walls as "an art, not a science." The stone came from the Hopeman Quarry along the Scottish coast.

The wood from the whisky barrels used to build the second-floor walls was originally twice as thick to hold the whisky, so it was split for the purposes of the build, with some of the spare wood being used for the interior. You can still see how thick the barrels originally were in the basement.

The barrel house is well insulated with 8-in (20-cm) Warmcel® insulation. According to Auriol, it is like "a little sauna" when she lights the wood-burning stove.

The roundness and irregularity of the building have meant that the carpenter was able to create beautiful cabinets and work surfaces, with every element becoming a piece in a giant jigsaw puzzle.

An attractive sculptural spiral staircase from the kitchen leads up to the bedroom landing, where Auriol maintains her privacy by hanging rugs over the railings. Each of the risers in the staircase contains five holes, which creates tiny views and windows of light from all angles. Climbing up the stairs, she comments, helps to keep her fit!

The barrel house is also a place of creativity. Auriol sews and writes poetry in the basement guest room. She had recently been asked to read at a Taizé Meditation and Peace Dance, and has been encouraged to write nature poems on a weekly basis. One of Auriol's favorite paintings is by Ted Roberts, who taught art with her.

ABOVE A spiral staircase leads to the bedroom, which is given privacy by hanging rugs over the handrails. Light filters in from all angles through the circular holes in the risers, giving the stairs an open and airy feel.

"My whisky barrel house is a flow of art, music, light, and energy. I feel in touch with every corner of it. It has an integrity that I enjoy."

Roger's whisky barrel house is located at The Findhorn Foundation (see page 34), in Forres, Scotland, in the same part of the community as Auriol's barrel house (see pages 126–29). It was the first to be built there and is smaller than Auriol's. Roger envisaged a cluster of whisky barrel houses and needed to persuade the Community Council to let him build them. The council felt that the houses might smell of good Scottish whisky, but this is not the case. They agreed on a prototype and he built this, making doors, windows, and an upstairs sleeping platform. He thought of it as a guesthouse for visitors, but moved in himself.

BELOW Roger has built a tiny whisky barrel house behind his current home, which he can use as an accessible bedroom when he finds that the stairs to his loft bedroom become too much.

The whisky barrels came from Fife, in Scotland. Whisky has a long history in Fife. The whisky-distilling roots of Lindores Abbey, in Newburgh on the north coast of Fife, can be traced back to 1494 when details of the malt duty paid by Friar John Cor were logged in the Exchequer Roll—the first written evidence of whisky distillation in Scotland.

Roger came to Findhorn in the early days and was inspired by its founders, Eileen and Peter Caddy and their friend Dorothy. The story of the garden next door to their caravan has become part of the founding myth. Eileen's spiritual beliefs included the concept of "the garden within" and being in touch with the angels of the plant kingdom. The angels told Eileen what to plant, how, when, and where. Eileen, Peter, and Dorothy all believed in co-operation between nature and mankind, nature spirits or the Davic Realms, and the divine or "God." Enormous vegetables were grown on what appeared to be poor land and the garden grew in fame. Today the garden and original caravan still exist. You enter the garden through a decorative rustic gate and it is still lush and productive.

Roger says that building "in the round" takes a lot more time, but there were a designer, a stonemason, and a professional joiner to help, as well as building volunteers. The whole build cost about £10,000 (US$ 13,000). For his 70th birthday, Roger gave himself a stained-glass window for the circular roof light.

Roger has built another even smaller whisky barrel shed behind his home for the time when he can no longer climb the ladder to his sleeping platform. This is currently his office. He says it would have cost about £65,000 (US$ 85,000) if he'd used paid labor.

The main barrel house has a wooden porch with a stone and slate floor, plus plenty of room for shoes and boots, plants, and "gubbins." As you enter, the main room has a large window, over which Roger has a curtain to ensure some privacy from those passing by on a path to a co-housing group. "Otherwise, it would be a room with a view!" he says.

ABOVE The rooflight is filled with color from a design made by a friend and the colorful light reflects around the room. The light moves around the space from morning until the last rays of the evening sun.

The interior cladding of the barrel house is redwood and the walls are insulated with 8-in (20-cm) thick Warmcel® insulation. There's also 6-in (15-cm) insulation in the roof to keep the house warm and cozy. He says that Auriol's barrel house is insulated better than his, but that his was the prototype.

The wood-burning stove provides the heating, but there's also an electric heater for especially cold Scottish winter nights. Enough wood used to come from the Foundation's own forest, but now it is partly

BELOW The main room is comfortable and opulent, with a deep red sofa and chair, and a wood-burning stove that uses logs from the local forest. The curtains add to the cozy atmosphere of Roger's sitting room.

bought in. Their own wood and bulk buying means that wood is not expensive for the residents.

There is a wall with Roger's precipitous steps to his bed next to his bookcase and behind the wall a tiny kitchen and bathroom with storage. His sitting room is well lived in and comfortable.

There was a concern at one time that The Findhorn Foundation was aging and that young people might not come. That they have is partly because of the community's ethos of creating a sustainable future, which demonstrates to others around the world that there are new ways to live and work, and this has an attraction—particularly in these times and partly because of a desire to live "tiny," sustainably, and in a community. As another resident said, "There are more baby buggy wheels than car wheels now!"

Roger knows more than most about the history of The Findhorn Foundation and how it works, and is one of many residents who take visitors on guided tours. Indeed, he was the first person we met for our own tour when he explained how the Foundation was the first Global Village, where people can learn and grow.

At The Findhorn Foundation, there is a mixture of eco-friendly and spiritual credentials, which gives the community coherence, with some people being more "eco" and some more spiritual. There is an acceptance of difference.

Roger says fondly of his whisky barrel house, "I get to live in a womb for the rest of my life."

ABOVE Next to the bookcase is the ladder to the bedroom which Roger feels might become too difficult to use one day but, for now, takes up little of the precious room.

"The Findhorn Foundation was the first Global Village, a place of sustainable living, learning, and spirituality—where each person seeks their own path and journey, is economically viable, and can attend courses and conferences."

The community at The Findhorn Foundation (see page 34) is eclectic, with huge variations in the size and style of the houses. These range from tiny wooden yurts to large, modern eco-houses. Most of the houses were built in the community's earliest days in organic and creative ways, including caravans and caravan-inspired designs, stone roundhouses, and the better-known whisky barrel houses.

Other initiatives, such as a co-housing development and the more recent developments on the East and West Whins, were spearheaded by associated companies/charitable trusts. The Centires Terraces were designed to accommodate one and two people as a more affordable way of being a part of the community. One of the Centires Terrace houses belongs to **Bryony and Liam.** Bryony had many friends at the Foundation. When her husband Liam's job took him to Scotland, they thought they wouldn't be able to afford to buy a home there, but one of the row (terraced) houses came on the market and, although tiny, it was "the only way to buy." The couple have a toddler and baby, so efficiency of space is of paramount importance. Liam's job and Bryony's osteopathy practice make this a busy home, combining working and bringing up children. The porch and a shed help maximize the available space.

Timber-framed and wood-clad, the house has a quirky, charming feel, with the personality of each house in the row being expressed through planting and decoration on and around the porches.

"The community, with its communal dining room and playgroup, as well as the opportunity to know lots of other people with young families, is a wonderful way to bring up children."

The heating comes from solar power and the solar Rotex store is in a cupboard in the porch area, which also provides space for coats and shoes. The Rotex, coupled with the insulation, means they never have to heat the upstairs and a hanging clothes dryer is rigged above the stairs. As Bryon says, "Somehow it works and it is very economical."

The one room upstairs includes a galley kitchen and a children's playpen in the sitting-room area. Their bedroom is on the ground floor, where they have their own bed and also the baby's cot. Opening the set of drawers in the room is not that easy! Their toddler, Ruben, has his own narrow room with a bunk bed with a tent covering.

The glass doors in the bedrooms and the large window upstairs let in lots of natural light, while the high upstairs ceiling gives a feeling of spaciousness to this busy little house. White walls also add to the feeling of space. Bryony says, "It is hard to get away from each other sometimes." But they have a garden to expand into when the weather is good, and there are also communal parks and gardens.

BELOW Upstairs is a large sitting room and partly divided-off kitchen area. In this high-ceilinged room with its amazing window, they have just enough room for their family of two children.

John was one of the early residents at The Findhorn Foundation, in Forres, Scotland (see page 34). In 1967 there was only "a collection of caravans and tents." He had a family and went away to teach. Being made redundant was "perfect", as he came back for a conference at Findhorn in 2002 on "Soul and Education"—and chose to stay. He has since worked in the Conference Office organizing conferences such as the upcoming conference on "Co-creative Spirituality" in 2018 and another in 2019 on "Climate Change and Consciousness."

John had the opportunity to build on the Field of Dreams, which is a part of The Findhorn Foundation, but didn't want to live in a box. Instead, he worked with an architect to design a hexagonal house based on bee honeycombs, to follow his passion for keeping bees. They called the house "The Honeypot." It has changed somewhat since then, when it suited his lifestyle, and since he met **Sylvie**. John and Sylvie found they needed more space. Indeed, Sylvie moving in began a new stage in their lives. When they met up, she would say to John, "It is ridiculous for me not to live in your home." So, they made new commitments for a life together.

Sylvie is a scenar therapist and needed a practice room. The house had been a creative and open-plan space, but this wasn't practical anymore. What was once a deck is now a new seating area. They had the kitchen extended for reasons of practicality and storage, and made it more beautiful. This was a challenge, as there isn't a right angle anywhere. Natural wood and supports against the soft white walls create a peaceful home. Sylvie says, "It took a while to get used to the shapes," but adds, "The beauty is in those shapes." This included the hexagonal table in the dining area.

RIGHT Originally this timber-clad house was hexagonal. When Sylvie moved in, John extended the house and created a terrace.

John has lived in both a five-bedroom house and a caravan, but comments, "It is not the size that makes our home a happy place." When the grandchildren come to stay, they put up tents in the garden and they have wonderful family meals on the deck. Their home is still compact, but it is cozy and works for them.

John describes how children were not welcome at Findhorn in the early years, but now there is a Steiner School, Children's Sanctuary, park and play areas, and more and more young people want to come here, or stay or return as a second generation. There are 35 nationalities from all over the world at Findhorn, reflecting its aim of being an international village. They are working toward a new paradigm of living, working, and being together.

The floors of the timber-framed building are made from hardwearing and sustainable bamboo, and the inside is painted with white eco-paint. Friends and family helped with the build. A geologist and artist friend designed an internal stone wall, which contains stones from each of the Scottish mountains John has climbed.

ABOVE Set against wood and stone, this rhomboid unit with stone shelves holds family pictures and decorative pieces.

TOP There are no right angles in this part of the house. Everything was handmade to fit, which took John and Sylvie some time to get used to. Now they enjoy the wood of the cabinets, countertops, and bamboo floor.

The main bedroom's ceiling, which has beams radiating from the center, reflects the house's hexagonal design and wooden furniture is placed against the angular walls. In this bedroom, red curtains and pelmets add color and texture. There is also a downstairs bedroom and a sofa bed, which means they "can get 6 adults in—squashed."

In the past, John and Sylvie have been able to use the resources of timber and wood thinning from Findhorn's forests. Now a 25 tonne wood delivery comes from a sustainable local Woodland Trust. They also have wind power at the community, getting enough energy from the Scottish winds to sell back to the United Kingdom's National Grid at times. There is a new Art Center that uses geo-energy, which draws up heat from the earth and increases it in a "reverse fridge" system. They have a wood-burning stove, passive solar gain from the double-glazed windows, and insulation, including a living roof. All this means that their heating bills are very small. "The Honeypot" house was complete. Then, as John says, "A swarm of bees came."

BELOW The downstairs bedroom is light, spacious, and airy, with white walls and a vaulted ceiling. The tall windows lead to the balcony beyond.

Tucked away down a small path through some trees at The Findhorn Foundation (see page 34), in Forres, Scotland, is **Dürton's** wooden "yurt." It is a wooden roundhouse with rustic steps up to the front door. This is home to Dürton, who had lived in shared housing for 17 years in Pineridge and in the Findhorn community for 25 years in all.

Dürton had shared houses before, but had become less keen on shared living and begun looking for an alternative. She waited for somewhere suitable at The Findhorn Foundation, and the yurt became available. It was located in the middle of the village and she had thought it might be too central. It was a time for some re-attunement.

Although Dürton enjoys living alone, she does not want to be completely isolated. She leaves her door open, so that visitors know that they are welcome. In fact, while we were there a young boy came in and was given caring attention. The mix of generations makes living here more fun. People in the community support each other and live

ABOVE Dürton's tiny wooden roundhouse is in the middle of The Findhorn Foundation Village, yet has a feeling of seclusion because it is set among the trees. A path leads away from the road to Dürton's home.

their lives in different ways. Dürton asks, "Do I want to be by myself or a part of others?" It seems she has achieved both, often—weather permitting—only closing the door at night. The garden around the yurt is unfenced, adding to the feeling of being a part of the wider community.

The roof of the yurt has a central circular glass window, which lets in plenty of light. Dürton comments that it needs cleaning from time to time because of the trees, which involves using a ladder to reach that high. She also put in extra windows and a glass front door to let in more light.

There is only a wood-burning stove, but, with plenty of insulation, this is good enough to keep the house warm. Dürton made many changes to the yurt to make it feel like home, including putting windows in the adjoining porch. Here, she has both a library and a room for her creative activities, which include sewing. She used rough-edged wood for the shelving. On a chair sits a small puppet, with a witch-like quality. Dürton says, "I have some of that in me, but I don't like labels or being "put into boxes."

The extra little room makes her home just big enough and all the difference when the rest of the living space is in one circular room in the yurt. She says, "I did it all." This includes everything in the garden that surrounds her home. She loves to chop firewood. The building and garden "keep me more on my toes." They require "more engagement with my life."

Dürton sleeps in an alcove with a lightweight curtain that she draws back during the day to create a seating area. There's storage space at one end of the bedroom area, with everything hidden behind a wooden wall from which hang a small harp and a guitar.

The kitchen units have been built to fit into one area; there is seating and a small, round table. There is also a bathroom, which she describes as "big for a boat."

Dürton has everything she needs in that one tiny yurt room, with its adjoining porch. It is where she socializes, sleeps, eats, and creates. The soft esthetic, with flowers, books, rugs, and throws, makes this an extremely friendly, cozy home. "I love small spaces," she says.

BELOW The main room contains a table and chairs, a kitchen area, and a curtained-off bedroom. The wood-burning stove, plus great insulation, keep Dürton cozy and warm.

When **Christine and Ted** moved to their current house in Norfolk, England, it was not as it is today. The barn "needed a great deal of pimping up." Indeed, her husband was not impressed until Christine took him to the top of the hill—an unusual feature in this part of the world—and showed him the view over the common to the River Tas. It also came with 9 acres (3.6 hectares), which meant that Christine could plant trees, grow her own food, and cultivate flowers for bees and other pollinators. Fortunately, he agreed.

The barn was substantially extended and modernized into a beautiful and creative home. Behind the barn is an enclosed courtyard that nestles against a steep hill. This is the way to the treehouse. Climbing up a flight of wooden steps set into the hillside you come out to the view and the treehouse. There is a spiral shower made of corrugated tin where hot water can be had via a heating system designed for washing horses and stables. Next to the shower is the treehouse.

Ted started building the treehouse and a builder came to finish it. Built on poles and supported by trees, there is a metal staircase with wooden handrails leading to a small landing area. The lower room is lined with pale tongue-and-groove paneling, which act as a neutral background for their art and colorful furniture. Christine says that they already had all the furniture found inside. They didn't want to spend money when they already had stuff in storage. Everything came from the shed—even the coat hooks. The question of "Why have we got all these old things?" was answered.

The old things included two small, mustard-colored chairs and a table, above which hangs a black-and-white picture of a treehouse— a present from a friend. A second impression of trees was created by another friend, with the picture looking straight up into the trees to produce a mandala-like design. The sofa was bought in an auction in Glasgow years ago and, as Christine comments, "It was nice to use it again." There's also a large ornate mirror from their home in Glasgow

ABOVE Christine and Ted's treehouse is built at the top of a very steep slope with steps set into the hillside to take them to the trees. This little home from home is built on tree trunks to give it more height and to take advantage of the great Norfolk views.

OPPOSITE The metal stairs and balustrade stringing give the treehouse a contemporary feel. From this side of the tiny house, there are further beautiful views down a more gentle slope over the fields.

"We are very happy for people to come and stay... I am about growing. Who I am is in my nine acres."

RIGHT The sleeping loft is minimal, with twin beds and views of the tops of the trees and the sound of birds at dawn and dusk.

that reflects the dappled, leafy green. The electric heater produces enough warmth in this double-glazed and insulated space to keep the treehouse snug and warm.

Built onto the main room is a veranda that is supported by the tall trees, where they can watch the sunsets through the foliage across the ancient common and over the hills. At night, one of the most haunting sounds is that of the barn owl

The corrugated tin theme is continued for the outside composting toilet. The metal, which contrasts with the natural space in which it sits, gives the loo a contemporary feel and reflects the colors around it.

Christine's treehouse has had many incarnations. It was once her son's home and he had TV and indulged in gaming until his parents cut off the electricity. The treehouse was originally intended to be "Ted's Folly," his shed, where he would have installed the piano if he could.

ABOVE The living room is decorated in white and pastels, providing a backdrop for Christine's furniture, all of which are favorite pieces.

After the treehouse had been their son's den, it was neglected for a while. It was renovated recently because Christine and Ted were thinking of starting with Airbnb, but they found getting comprehensive insurance a problem and didn't want to take any risks. They could put in a microwave, but for now are happy to cook out of doors, underneath the treehouse. It is currently used by guests and for special occasions. "We are very happy for people to come and stay." In terms of their future plans, Christine is open, saying, "We'll get there."

Apart from the orchard, Christine planted everything between the house and the little barn. In the last 15 years, the trees have matured and wild flowers and orchids now grow next to the paths that meander through the land. A mature tree tunnel opens up to reveal the rolling hills and the view over the garden to Christine's potting shed. This building has a rustic veranda that is lined with pots of flowers, and a room with a cooker, table and chairs, and two cat baskets. Perhaps it's a "tiny home" for cats?

BELOW From the living space a door leads to the balcony, which is supported by tall trees so Christine and Ted can enjoy the lovely views.

Down a lane in England's Norfolk are several shacks and sheds. **George** lives in one of these, having bought 4 acres (1.6 hectares) of land. At first, he lived in another shack, enjoying this life of self-reliance for over four years before being able to live lawfully in his new home. The total cost of the build and various additions was £2,140 (US$ 2,800). Solar power, electricity, and a bathtub brought the building cost up to £3,000 (US$ 4,000). Due to UK law, George had to prove he had lived there for four years—he found two witnesses and a receipt from a truck hire company to do this. He now hopes his grandson will come and stay, and sleep in the loft space when he is old enough.

George explains that the building was a solution to a personal problem. He thinks more people could live this low-impact, low-money lifestyle, believing that the low energy costs of shack-living are also a solution for the global community. He has just one solar panel that charges large batteries to provide electric light.

There was originally just one shack and then George built a second one. This one is, George says, more interesting. It was previously a shed for 10 years. The main structural poles were creosoted to ensure they would last and the rafters were made from local ash trees without being squared-off. Some oak thinnings from his woods were used to make window casements and uprights. These were squared off using an axe and planer.

The walls were made from boarding filled with hemp lime. The boarding was shuttered to build the walls up from the ground. This involved using wooden shuttering or boards, which were fixed to the uprights and then filled with the hemp lime. This is a flexible and practical material, with good thermal properties. He is proud that only one bag of cement was needed in the build; otherwise, all the materials were gleaned locally, including wood from a local sawmill. The walls are insulated with sheep's wool.

Plastering the walls with lime and sand, using soaked sacking to fill in holes, and then painting with unslaked lime mixed with cooking oil gives a lumpy effect, which George likes. He says this is a Roman recipe.

George explains, "I resist having my time valued. I take time making adjustments, using my hands to build silently without machinery." He comments that, in this day and age, we are being educated for helplessness and not being at home in the world. As George says, "There was a time when I could fix everything!"

ABOVE George lives in a shack, which he built himself using timber and limecrete, in wooded surroundings with an apple orchard. He has a kiln for his pottery and chickens run freely around the place.

LEFT The shack is a tiny, unprepossessing, one-roomed home. Inside there are a table, chairs, a wood-burning stove and kettles. A bed tucked behind a sofa, plus all the outbuildings, meet George's other needs.

Hidden away in a Norfolk field is a Mongolian yurt, or ger, that **Firefly and Johann** found online in Wales. It is home to them and their baby, Kai. In summer, it nestles amid the foliage of apple trees and the connection with nature is profound for this young couple.

Everything in the yurt's structure is traditional, from the canvas covering to the wooden struts, which are painted a bright red and have what Johann calls "squiggles" that he doesn't particularly like. Many Mongolian yurts integrated Buddhist symbolism in their designs, structure, and proportions, which are based on those in Buddhist temples.

The yurt is open-plan, with a dividing set of shelves. The kitchen feels spacious and there are cupboards, shelves (which Firefly designed from old drawers), and a wooden work surface that had to be cut to fit into the curve of the yurt.

LEFT The solar panels on the yurt are lowered in winter in order to catch the lower sun. When Firefly and Johann were expecting their baby Kai, they built the extension using recycled materials.

BELOW The yurt blends into the trees, looking like a giant mushroom. Army-grade tarpaulins cover and insulate the roof and a large, red-painted window adds a splash of vibrant color.

Inside, the window is framed by potted plants next to a beautiful chair draped with a sheepskin; a table and chairs fit between the door and the window. Due to the high-domed roof, nowhere feels cramped. Firefly, a photographer, has a desk and the rest of the space has a sofa, which used to belong to Johann's great-grandmother, and a huge bean-bag on a rug.

The wood-burning stove, with its many kettles, sits in the center of the yurt surrounded by fireguards to protect little Kai as he crawls around the floor.

From outside the yurt has a dark, organic feel because it has been covered with insulation. Another layer of insulation, a low-grade army surplus canvas, protects the yurt from the English weather.

ABOVE The yurt is a traditional Mongolian yurt with the "Eye of Heaven" bringing in light. The flue of the wood-burner chimney rises through the opening in the roof. The struts are painted bright red with an ornate Mongolian pattern.

The structure is made of closely spaced struts that rest on uprights and then slot into the wheel structure at the top of the dome, which is sometimes called "The Eye of Heaven" or, more traditionally, the "toonoo." This lets in light, and Johann and Firefly have also put in a large window to bring in more light. The frame was built and fitted, with the canvas "tucked in." The red door is small and traditional, with a handle of found wood.

Johann and Firefly built the base of the yurt to be robust, insulated, and mouse-free, then laid a wooden floor in quarters. The wood, which was recycled from a massive cable drum, was planed to be of a consistent size and finished with linseed and Danish oils. It was laid over plywood and made in sections to fit, which was "quite a challenge." Materials have come from dumpsters or skips and Freecycle offers.

They live off-grid with a water-collection system, composting toilets, and solar panels. The solar panels have winter and summer angles. In the winter, the panels catch the lower sun and, at the same time, create a porch where they keep wood, while the panels are lifted onto the roof in the summer, so opening the yurt to the outside world when the door is left open.

Johann, Firefly, and baby Kai sleep in a cabin next door, which they built themselves and where they installed a wood-burning

"It's not an easy life in some ways... we need to keep on top of the maintenance of filters, chop wood, collect water, and keep the inside from going into chaos."

BELOW Firefly and Johann soon realized that Kai would need a bedroom of his own, so they built another room using natural materials and added a negatively stenciled wall of trees to reflect the view outside.

stove and shower. The shower has a lovely wooden carved screen. There is storage space under the bed and old suitcases sitting on a high shelf provide further storage. A recess in the white, tongue-and-grooved wall holds their Buddha.

Johann has learnt to plumb and build with the wonderful help of friends, their brothers, the Internet, and books. This re-skilling is part of their ethos for living a more mindful life and living it without the strictures of mainstream living. They also enjoy being part of an environment that they are caring for themselves. Firefly says that she feels empowered by taking part in the build, especially that of the cabin, which they constructed from scratch.

Living as they do is hard work, with lots of chores needing to be done each day, but there are many benefits for Firefly and Johann. There is the closeness of nature; of owls such as little owls, tawny owls, and barn owls (plus the raucous calls from a nearby rookery); and of the seasons and weather. There is the freedom to do anything they like, from moving the wood-burner to a better position or building shelves. Firefly can't imagine "living in a box." Johann and Firefly want to show others that living in this way is possible.

The idea of having land and a house they had built together grew on married couple **Andy and Ella** for a long time. After they found some land, near Glastonbury, in England's Somerset, they had a bit of a battle getting planning permission to build their timber-framed house there. However, they changed the concept to a strawbale house, which the planners looked on favorably, and their design was accepted. As Andy remarks, "They generally like something special... it ticks a box." And Andy and Ella were keen to make it special.

At first, they lived in some stables on the land. These occupied 527 square feet (49 square meters). Andy and Ella knew that they didn't need more space—just something better arranged. The foundations of their strawbale house rest on a stone plinth overlaid with beams, OSB

ABOVE This beautiful strawbale house, in Somerset, is based at the permaculture center that Andy runs. It was a building made with love by Andy and his late wife, Ella, and also by many helpers wanting to gain experience with this type of building.

(Oriented Strand Board), heater bricks, a layer of clay and sand, and recycled bitumen fiberboard with battens fixed above filled with 8in (20cm) of natural sheep's wool. The floor then forms the final layer. It can be very cozy inside, unless the temperature drops to 14°F (-10°C) for many days, in which case they light the wood-burning stove. Their home then heats up very quickly. The thermal mass and insulation is enough to keep it warm. Andy says, "It's like a storage heater." Indeed, the whole building holds the heat and, on hot summer days, the roof lights have to be opened to cool it down.

The straw bales were stacked between framing poles and then plastered with a clay mix. Other people came to help to gain experience of the process. They enjoyed working together while they were learning, which Andy says was very satisfying. The poles are wonderfully straight and knot-free, as they came from thinnings from larch trees grown for ships' masts.

The roof was finished with oak tiles called "shakes." These came from local oak trees that were being cut down, and many hours were spent cutting and shaping them. Andy says the tiles should last for more than 100 years, as well as being objects of beauty next to the solar panels. Andy and Ella originally wanted a living roof, but were not sure about the load-bearing capacity of the strawbale house. The frame was made with round wood, as it is stronger than sawn wood and also looks

RIGHT The veranda wraps around the side of the building with lovely views over the trees. After Ella died, Andy felt comforted that her hands had smoothed out the plaster and felt that her presence was in everything that they had achieved together.

better. They got in a structural engineer who assured them that their design would take three times the weight of the roof they had planned, and it has, indeed, turned out to be a solid structure.

Although Andy is a carpenter, he commissioned the help of another carpenter to make the frame; otherwise, he says, "I built the house myself." The frame is made of Douglas fir using traditional pegging to fix it in place. They were going to drive the pegs home, but Ella pointed out that the protruding pegs would be great for hanging up washing and other paraphernalia. If the pegs become loose, they can be driven in, but they are sound and stay put, which gives the poles character.

Coming down a path through the permaculture gardens, you reach the door to the house. Just inside the entrance, there are shelves for boots and shoes. For the stone floor in this part of the living space, Andy got the slabs from the same local quarry that supplied the stones for the plinth foundation. The stone flags show natural iron patterns from ancient water. It is naturally layered and he hasn't treated it in any way. He comments, "We liked that." The rest of the floor is made from local wood that was milled nearby. The wood was laid out and both air- and kiln-dried in a large barn by a firm called Land Logic. The whole

BELOW Andy made the sofa from an old bed. There is a wood-burning stove and underfloor heating, which is rarely used, as the building is so well-insulated.

RIGHT There are many wood features in the structure and furnishings of the house, such as the larch-wood shelves. In the kitchen the countertops are made from Douglas fir.

floor is laid over underfloor heating, but this is hardly ever used in this well-insulated and thermally sound house. They were able to use the slab wood off-cuts in places such as the veranda and overhang, which Andy found satisfying because he could use the whole tree.

There is a living space, office, bedroom, bathroom, and kitchen area. The interior walls are wattle and daub with a clay-lime mix. Wattle and daub is a composite building material used for making walls, in which a woven lattice of wooden strips called wattle is daubed with a sticky material usually made of some combination of wet soil, clay, sand, animal dung, and straw.

In the main room there's a large sofa, which Andy adapted from an old bed. Wooden bookcases run along a wood and glass partition wall and there is also a table and chairs. Indeed, there are many wonderful wooden features throughout this inviting home, including in the kitchen, where the countertops are made from Douglas fir and the shelves from larch wood. Through a beautifully carved arched door is their bedroom, which is separated from the main living space by the partition wall.

What gives Andy the most satisfaction is that he made this wonderful home himself with the help of Ella and also of friends when necessary.

Marcus lives in a roundhouse in a clearing, reached down a long track through some woods in Somerset, England. There is also a small shed on stilts for an organization called World Wide Opportunities on Organic Farms (WWOOF). There's a workshop where he is creating a potential space for additional sleeping and living. The surrounding area supports one-third of the last culm grass moorland growing in the world, a grass that once covered much of Devon.

Marcus describes himself as a once itinerant woodsman and he lived in a caravan for 17 years. He was born in Somalia and his father was involved in forestry and game in Malawi, so Africa is in his heart. It was the experience of seeing the traditional round rondavels that inspired him to build his own roundhouse. As a kid he, like many of us, loved making dens. He says, "I just got better at it." His dream was to live in a roundhouse and he adds, "It is weird to go into a square house."

Marcus has worked with wood and in forestry and conservation most of his life, including in England's Exmoor National Park. His dream was to work for himself and buy some land. He had £60 (US$ 80) when his woodland came up for sale and was given two months to come up with

BELOW When Marcus found the woodland in which he now lives, the design for his roundhouse was shaped by his Buddhist philosophy and beliefs, the environment, and the materials, including the wood, which nearly all came from the surrounding 20 acres.

ABOVE All the wood for Marcus' wood-burning stove comes from the nearby woods and is stored around the walls and beneath the eaves of the living roof.

"I try to inspire people and teach by example. It's the important act of re-skilling others."

the money. He began teaching woodland skills. At first only nine people came and then 90. By the March of that year, he had come up with the money. Working and saving finally got him there.

The plan for the roundhouse "was released out of my head." Most of the wood came from the surrounding 20 acres (8 hectares), was recycled, or, necessary, bought from sustainable sources. Marcus milled the wood himself.

Nevertheless he had some criteria—a round table, which is more civilized, a sofa, and a decent bed were the basis of his requirements. He made the sofa and the bed, which he hides behind a large "Tree of Life" cloth. As the sun moves around the roundhouse, its rays create patterns on the wall from which Marcus can tell the time. His drums and colorful African wall hanging reflect his love of Africa.

The entrance to the porch room has an arched roof built from naturally curved wooden struts, which dictated its pleasing shape. As Marcus didn't want to cook in the main room, the kitchen is there, with every cabinet and shelf made from local woodland timber, including burr oak. This use of natural materials throughout makes Marcus's home a living, breathing place of warmth and creative beauty. The porch room has a flagstone floor and the main room a wooden floor. The porch faces south, as would be traditional in a Mongolian yurt.

In the center of the main room is a wood-burning stove beneath the "Eye of Heaven," through which the chimney flue rises. Marcus describes the sacred meanings of a traditional roundhouse, in which the center represents the center of the universe. The stove, surrounded by a decorative design that's painted on the wooden floor, sits on a huge circle of slate. This was a luxury that nearly didn't happen, not least because its size almost prevented him getting it through the door.

The roof was made of 1/4 in. (4-mm) plywood, with two layers overlapping for strength and sitting on poles, which were originally intended for a tee-pee and were long enough for a very wide span. Set closely together and resting on the ash lattice, traditional to yurts, they give additional strength to the roof. Marcus says, "It's a basket." The roof has two layers of carpet, layed pile to pile. Under the carpets is a pond liner, which weatherproofs the roof. Marcus, finally, chucked a

ABOVE Kettles sit on the wood-burning stove, ever ready with hot water to provide for cooking and tea-making.

LEFT The design is built on the principles of a Mongolian yurt with the center of the room—featuring the wood-burning stove, which sits on a circle of slate, and the "Eye of Heaven"— representing the center of the universe.

mixture of grit and compost over the roof suitable for growing sedum plants, which are very hardy in all weathers. This feature, apart from being beautiful and blending the roof with nature, adds insulation. He says, "The worms and other plants arrived with the birds."

The outer wood cladding is insulated with sheep's wool and fixed together with cable ties, but these are not what keep the building standing up. The outside is red cedar, which has its own fungicidal and insecticidal properties. It is the lattice attached to a long tension band that holds the building together. It prevents the natural outward stress of the roof by binding the lattice and preventing spread. This is traditional in yurt-building, and Mongolian and other yurts often have a decorative band anchored to the door frame. Marcus's band was probably used to lift boats out of the water at a quayside for the maintenance and repair of ships. It was a great find.

About a quarter of the roof around the "Eye of Heaven" is clad with shingle tiles. Marcus considered making enough to cover the whole roof, but his experience of roofing the shed with shingle told him it would be impossible and he didn't want to do it again.

It took a seven-year-long battle with the local council to get planning permission for his roundhouse, on the understanding that it could be taken apart. Eventually, they left him alone. "It was a learning curve for them," he says. Having a plant nursery (the whole area is a nursery based on permaculture design) and burning charcoal were contributing factors to his success. Now he pays Council Tax, for which he gets his garbage collected.

Marcus has worked hard to achieve this home and a place to pass on wood skills to young people. He can't sell the roundhouse if he ever leaves, but he can leave it to his children.

BELOW Marcus has built a porch at the entrance of the roundhouse, which is also his kitchen. The roof follows the natural lines of the structural arch and all the units are made from local wood, including burr oak.

LEFT When John wanted to create a covered area between the yurt and the caravan, it provided an opportunity to build a beautiful and useful space. John and Mary call this the "conservatory," and it has storage, a bench, and wonderful plants beyond the lovely organic archway.

RIGHT John and Mary's home is set in the beautiful Somerset landscape. When the weather is fine, they can eat outside or simply enjoy nature, which means so much to them both.

Hidden away through some gardens is a gate, beyond which is **John and Mary's** pretty home where they live with their daughter. Their life there started with a 1991 Roma Supreme caravan, a caravan often used by gypsies and traveling people. They had been WWOOFing (World Wide Opportunities on Organic Farms) in an orchard in Somerset, England, when they discovered that they could park up there, plus John also became a permanent helper. At first, they lived in the caravan and then bought the yurt from Avalon Yurts. They found that going from the yurt to the caravan and back was often cold, wet, and muddy, so John made a covered decking area between the two spaces, using corrugated plastic to let in the light. As John explains, "We stopped wearing raincoats and boots."

John made an arched entrance porch to the decked area from natural wood and also shelves on either side for storing boots and other paraphernalia. The outside of the caravan and porch area is clad in naturally wavy lapped wood.

Building everything, including all the furniture and fittings, for the caravan was important to John. He says, "For me, building my own home and being connected to it is most profound and contributes to my humanity and experiences." They have enough power from the solar panels on the roof, except during six weeks around the time of the Winter Solstice when they use a generator if necessary.

LEFT John and Mary added the yurt when they began to feel too cramped in the caravan and when they felt able to settle down in the lovely fields around them.

OPPOSITE They created a bedroom in the yurt for themselves and their daughter whose bed John made as a "top bunk." The cloths behind the struts give this space an exotic and luxurious feel.

Living in this way wasn't new to John who has only ever lived in caravans and benders (simple structures made from arched poles of hazel or willow covered with blankets, felt, and waterproof sheets). As John says, "I was used to living in small spaces." He and Mary had their daughter and both felt they were meant to be in their roundhouse. The feeling of being on, and helping, the land was deep and profound. They say, "We have formed a bonding relationship with the land that we don't want to break... the land needs us."

John doesn't like the right angles and conventional materials used for most houses, preferring the roundness of the yurt and the curves, colors, and patterns of natural wood. He explains, "When I visit 'normal' houses I realize that there is no connection to nature but, as a human animal living here, it is so much healthier... more grounded, open-hearted, and happier."

The yurt is insulated with recycled carpet and all the wood for the wood-burning stove comes from their woodland. Everything is natural and the yurt "breathes." The yurt's shape and the fact that it has no corners are very calming. The roof is lined with an array of pink- and red-themed hangings behind the roof poles that radiate out from the "Eye of Heaven" in the center of the yurt.

The kitchen and dining space is in the caravan, with a seating area that looks out onto the "conservatory," and there is also a small study at the far end. The whole space is full of pictures, family photos, and drawings, giving it a homely feel.

Living in a small home has created some personal challenges for Mary and John, but they see this as an opportunity for deepening their relationship. What helps is having more than one space and the outdoor life. In winter they can get a bit of cabin fever, but in summer their place comes into its own, with outdoor eating, working, and living. They say, "Living a simple life frees the mind and spirit to focus on other things."

"We enjoy how we live before anything else... our lives outside and the creativity mean we are involved in every process and nothing is at odds here. We are connected to all of our choices."

Chapter five
COTTAGES AND HOUSES

Houses have been tiny for millennia, many having originally been built as workers' cottages or almshouses for the poor, and these can still be found in many towns and villages in the UK. There are three examples in this chapter, including an almshouse in Glastonbury, in Somerset, which has been furnished as it might have looked in days gone by. Another almshouse belongs to two artists, Annette and Mike, who were searching for somewhere to call home when they were accepted by the Trust managing the row of almshouses in which they now live. When Jo wanted to move to the country with her three daughters, she found a tiny old house that was once intended for local estate workers.

Julie's tiny house in a Suffolk town was too small to accommodate her art practice until a local brewery let her have some space elsewhere as a studio, although she has also turned her tiny back room into a small, but more accessible, studio.

Towns and villages across the UK used to have a great many pubs and inns, as well as coaching inns for travelers journeying by coach and horses in the days before trains and then cars and buses took over. Wendy's little cottage in Suffolk was once part of a coaching inn, and the old pub sign can still be seen on one of the houses in her row.

Carol and John's eco house has been a journey, as the design, use, and care of their home has evolved over time. Katy and Ollie's small strawbale roundhouse is both an eco-build and a tiny house, all of which they built themselves. Ollie is a master carpenter and woodsman who created everything with great care out of local wood, while Katy helped with the build and put her artistic skills into the striking sculptural details.

Jo and her three daughters live in an old estate cottage on the Helmingham Estate in England's Suffolk. It isn't an almshouse, as these were built specifically for the poor; rather the estate cottages were built for working families. She moved to her house from Ipswich 15 years ago in the dead of winter. The long, dark nights caused a friend to comment, "What have you done?" There were three days of painting before she and her girls could move in. It was freezing and they didn't know how to light a fire. As there is no central heating, they rely on their wood-burning stove for warmth, although it can be hard work tending it.

As Jo and the three girls acclimatized to their new home, they explored the gardens and cleared a tangle of brambles.

ABOVE The doors to all the houses are exactly the same, with ornate original ironwork, but Jo and her family prefer to use the entrance to the rear of the house.

TOP Jo's estate cottage used to house workers for the local landowner. It is one of a row of pretty homes, each with a small front garden.

They now have chickens, a polytunnel, and a vegetable garden. Jo works and looks after the girls, sometimes with the help of their grandmother, so she is very busy.

Jo's home is one of 15 beautiful little houses that were built for workers on the estate. The estate cottages, as well as the school in the village of Framsden, were designed 150 years ago by Lord John Tollemache of Helmingham Hall. Each cottage is paired and appears to be symmetrical but, as Jo says, there are differences, especially on the inside of the houses. The current Lady Tollemache is a world-renowned garden designer. The gardens at Helmingham are a tribute to her vision and design, and are open to the public in the summer.

ABOVE Jo has a much larger garden than most in the row of houses, where she keeps chickens, has a den, and grows vegetables. She also has a colorful cottage flower garden.

LEFT Jo has a studio behind the rear entrance of the cottage. In between the studio and the house would have been a pig house from the days when each cottage tenant was given a pig.

"I am very lucky to have a huge garden with a massive shed—it's bigger than the house—where the children can hang out and play."

LEFT A small private room, located off the sitting room, acts as a den and music room for Jo and her daughers.

BELOW The sitting/dining room has a red brick wall, table and chairs, and a comfy sofa. From the window are views across to the fields on the other side of the road.

In the past, two cottages would have shared a bread oven, and each had an acre of land to grow food for the family and to fatten a pig. These quaint cottages, once home to working families, are now mostly rented privately. Even so, Jo says, some are still "tied" to the Helmingham Estate, where the residents continue to have a working role and are likely to remain in their little houses when they retire.

Jo is fortunate to have a huge garden with a shed. She shares the garden with a neighbor and it is the largest in the row of cottages. There is a small studio and another shed for storing gardening tools. The garden slopes gently up the hill behind the house and in front of the cottages there's a pretty cottage garden and a path to the original arched front door with its ornate hinges. They never use the front door, but instead go around the back. The back door is next to a little yard where, in times gone by, the family would keep a pig. Jo says that in the past workers were encouraged to use the back doors, as to be seen "chatting" on the front doorstep was frowned upon. Jo's unused front door is curtained to prevent drafts and is at the bottom of the stairs to the eaves.

There is a sitting room with a dining table and chairs, and a view through the window to the hill on the other side of the road. The box room houses a piano and there is a kitchen and bathroom to the rear by the back door.

Upstairs there is a bed on the landing behind the balustrade and the girls were able to choose their own colors for their rooms in the eaves. There are jolly walls of turquoise, blue, and pink, each expressing the individuality of the occupant.

Now Jo can happily say, "I love living here out in the country and I want to stay."

ABOVE From the porch, at the back of the house, are the kitchen and bathroom. A collection of blue and white plates decorates the walls.

"There is no central heating and the heating we do have comes from a wood-burning stove with a back boiler set into a brickwork fireplace—so, it's hard work."

From the street, in the Conservation Area of Bury St Edmunds, in Suffolk, England, you can see a row of tiny houses. **Julie** lives in one of these. Her street is part of a medieval grid, but her house was built later—probably about 1875. It is one of a row of one-room-wide houses.

The area had a workhouse for the destitute from 1784. This building originally belonged to Jesus College and was founded in the 15th century to supply priests for Bury St Edmunds Abbey. Excavations have revealed the remains of a cellar, while the ruins of the Abbey sit in beautiful gardens in the nearby town.

ABOVE Although Julie has a studio, which was generously provided by a local brewery, she has converted a tiny back room into another studio for doing smaller scale artwork.

Julie is a painter and, when looking for a studio, met with the Greene King brewery nearby who have been making beer and running pubs for about 200 years. They were very helpful and offered Julie the use of an old carpenter's workshop for a peppercorn rent. They had no expectations of her and this gave her the freedom to make larger works away from home. "They've been amazing!" she says. This has been her studio for 13 years.

For Julie the little brick house is a place of transition, for being alone, learning how to feel safe, and being herself. It is her retreat.

Unusually, there is a parking space behind the row of little houses and, though there is no garden, the approach to Julie's house is filled with flowers in pots and there's enough room for a table and chair.

The house is one room's width—the widest part of the house being at the front and ever narrowing as you approach the rear, where there's a kitchen off the little hall. That and the upstairs room, in which Julie now paints, form the narrowest part of the house.

There are bountiful paintings and objects of beauty on the white walls throughout; many are Julie's own paintings and photo-prints. Some are very large, making no apology to the small rooms. The stair walls are also covered with pictures. This house may have begun simply and has order, but is not the house of a minimalist. The sitting room is accented with her large, colorful paintings, fabrics, and rugs. By the window that looks out onto the street at the front of the house, there's a table for Julie's computer. The window is a work of art in itself, with a hanging frame holding a cobweb of objects above a selection of other ornaments, which include iridescent blue bottles and a bowl of shells and feathers.

LEFT As time went by, Julie began to fill her house with her paintings and prints. These now cover most of the walls and add color to the stairs up to her bedroom and little studio.

There are toys under the stairs and on the landing for a visiting little one and at the top of the stairs is her "shrine"—a table of important objects and images on the walls.

Julie's bedroom is at the front of the house, looking onto the street. A pink flamingo stands comically in the window and her colorful paintings enliven this room too.

She recently began using the back bedroom for her work, although Greene King still allows her to keep the studio in the carpenter's workshop. She manages to fit in two easels and a table to work on. She says, "It works."

At first it was difficult to settle in and feel grounded. She needed to get away from constantly having people in her space. With a busy life nursing and looking after elderly people—which she enjoys—and a "crowded" past, her retreat is vital to her.

Now it is a place of comfort and beauty. Julie has started painting patterns on the wall in the hall. "It was quite a thing to draw and paint on the wall... to make it rich."

As Julie says, "The house is the story."

ABOVE The bedroom faces a street in Bury St Edmunds. A pink flamingo stands proudly on the windowsill.

BELOW The house is narrower at the back than the front, where Julie has a sitting room with paintings on the wall.

In a pretty little village in Suffolk, England, set well back from the road, is a row of almshouses. These Grade II listed buildings were built in 1575 and are now owned by The Elizabeth, Lady Cornwallis Almshouse Trust. They were built in memory of Elizabeth's daughter who died young. The properties managed by the Trust, which was set up for the benefit of the aged until the Trustees widened its scope in 2003.

Annette and Mike are lucky to have one of the almshouses, as the Trust only allows people who are "needy and worthy" to live there. They had been unable to get a council house and had been renting. They had a tiny income from their work as artists and were desperate not to be homeless. They applied to the Trust, without having much hope, but when the Trustees interviewed them they were accepted.

The cottages are very quaint and many original features, such as the beams, are exposed. For some time during the 1980s and '90s, the cottages were very run down, but they have gradually been improved over the last 15 to 20 years. There is one boiler serving all of the almshouses and the heating comes on at the same time for everyone.

Annette is a printmaker and fabric designer, making lamps, printing lino-cut designs on clothes, and producing hand-printed cards. She uses cats, hares, and other motifs from nature. A folding table opens up as a "studio," though Annette has further space with other craftspeople in a

ABOVE Annette and Mike were very fortunate to be accepted as residents of this ancient row of almshouses, which were originally intended for the poor. They couldn't afford a house, but the Trustees liked them and so they have a home in a Suffolk village.

"I think the residents enjoy the peace and community. The village is lively with communal events, lunches, and coffee mornings. There are people of all ages and lots going on."

co-operative studio in a nearby town. There she can make and sell her creations, as well as take her work to craft and design fairs. Former bookseller Mike is now a painter and also draws. He has moved from contemporary subjects to animal painting. His easel is set up in their bedroom and he stores paintings and canvases in the garden shed.

A hallway leads to the living room downstairs, which has a kitchen alcove. The beams, inglenook fireplace, and leaded windows are all original. The relatively high ceilings make the room feel larger. The window upstairs is the original leaded one, like the one downstairs. Annette says," I love that bedroom." She feels it is spacious enough for both of them, even with the easel and lack of storage. Annette and Mike both live and work together and, although they sometimes get in each other's way, the arrangement works well. They have learnt to compromise. The winters are cozy and warm, and the house becomes a nest.

BELOW At the moment, Mike paints by a window in the bedroom, but would love a studio in the garden one day.

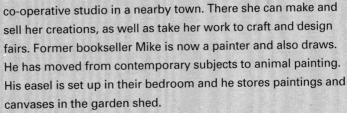

RIGHT The tiny sitting room has a sofa and table next to the kitchen alcove, where Annette can work at her printing designs when she isn't at her studio in Diss, Norfolk, at the "Designer Makers" collective of studios.

RIGHT AND BELOW The tiny
courtyard garden provides an
important extra "room" for
Wendy, where she can
entertain and grow plants in
pots against trellis. The shed
at one end of the garden
provides another retreat from
the tiny cottage.

Wendy's attractive little cottage is situated in a street in Eye, in the county of Suffolk, England. It is called April Cottage. Apparently, there were once 22 pubs in this small market town. Now there is only one. There are also the remains of a castle. There was a large coaching inn for travelers catching the Norwich to London coaches and a smaller one. Wendy's cottage is part of the smaller of the two old inns. The inn was built in around 1851 and was called the King's Head.

The archway where the horses and coaches used to stop is now the entrance to a small car parking space and also Wendy's small garden. In the summer, this is her extra room for dining, reading, gardening, and relaxing. The walls and high fences are lined with roses, clematis, foxgloves, buddleia, and other luscious plants, some of which climb up and over trellises.

"I love to sit outside in the evening, where the trees behind the cottage are a reminder of the countryside. I am happiest in my tiny garden and the work I put in repays me."

Off the garden is a tiny kitchen. Wendy finds that everyone just comes in through the back door. She enjoys entertaining and either uses the space outside or the kitchen, simply pulling out a table for very small gatherings of people. The kitchen is light and bright, with a window to the garden, Dutch (stable) doors, and lovely pops of bright red in the shades (blinds) and accessories.

Wendy explains there is also a cellar—blocked off in her house—which used to house the beer pumps for the pub. A previous owner found the cellar when doing renovation work and discovered that it ran along all the houses in the street. One of the houses still has access to this cellar. On the red brickwork on the outside of one of the cottages, there's the faint trace of a large painted sign, with white lettering on a green background. It says: "Lacon's Ales & Spirits"—Lacon's being brewers from the coastal Suffolk town of Great Yarmouth.

Wendy has lived in large houses in the past, including a farmhouse. The last house she lived in with her husband before he died was small, but not as small as this one. Yet she feels safe in the town, with neighbors who know her and finds that "people help each other."

In the mornings she can get up and fetch the newspaper, almost from next door, and there is an independent butcher, cafés, and stores all within a short walk. She has a car, but doesn't use it much.

RIGHT Wendy's little house is one of three that used to be a pub. The faded Lacon's sign on one of the other houses can still be seen here. The entrance to Wendy's house at the back is through a large archway, formerly used by coaches and horses.

Wendy loves sitting outdoors in the evening, finding that the trees behind the cottage remind her of the countryside. Wendy enjoys gardening and the tiny garden makes her very happy. She feels amply rewarded for all the work she puts into it. There is a gardening society in the town and Wendy sings in a local choir. She also enjoys the community spirit of the Wednesday Markets when local people bring produce to sell and there is a pop-up café serving tea, coffee, and cake. The markets have a gentle air of friendliness, while the competitions for the best plants and vegetables create a lively stir.

Wendy enjoys collecting photographs of her family and has many paintings, mostly of rural scenes and nature. An ornate mirror reflects the light in her sitting room, where many of these painting hang. Next to her mirror is a painting of anemones, which Wendy is particularly fond of, by the pre-war artist Winifred Walker, who was a fellow of the Royal Horticultural Society. Although this room is full of her things, it also has high ceilings, which is unusual in small cottages, and might be due to its pub heritage.

Paintings also line the staircase, at the top of which sit piles of books waiting for a floor-to-ceiling bookcase to accommodate them all.

Wendy's bedroom overlooks the street and is feminine and light, with paintings of flowers and her collection of colorful jewelry. On the

"I found it difficult to let go of some important pieces of furniture, such as my grandfather's desk... sadly, lots had to go to auction"

LEFT Off the little kitchen leading to the garden is Wendy's sitting room with many paintings and the ornaments and photographs she loves so much.

other side of the landing, there's another bedroom that has just enough room for a bed and side table for when her son comes to stay.

Wendy loves her little cottage, although when she left her previous home, she found it hard to dispose of some pieces of furniture that were important to her, such as her grandfather's desk and another piece from which her other grandfather used to serve drinks. Sadly, a lot of her precious pieces of furniture had to go to auction.

ABOVE The little kitchen has a breakfast bar and a Dutch (stable) door. This frames the view, on fine days, of Wendy's garden and the trees beyond.

"Everyone comes in through the back door. I love to entertain, either outside or in the kitchen, when I pull out a table for very small gatherings."

Katy and Ollie had a stroke of luck. They had met John and Carol through permaculture training and lived in the same area of Norfolk, England. John and Carol (see pages 184–87) had land at "The Hollow," which used to be an old chalk quarry and then an orchard. They had built a strawbale house and wanted others to be able to build sustainable ecological homes, too. They had one more plot left, with

ABOVE Katy and Ollie have a beehive on the roof. They enjoy beekeeping, along with John and Carol, as a part of their permaculture beliefs and way of living.

planning permission for a large strawbale house. It was a plot with mature walnut trees from the old orchard, as well as other tree species and hedges. Originally, they had thought about building a meditation center, but then their new idea took hold. They wondered what kind of person they would like to build there and thought of Katy and Ollie. They visited Katy and Ollie's with a bunch of cucumbers and sealed the deal. Although Katy and Ollie don't own the land, they have been able to build their home there. They can live there for as long as they wish, as this fits in with John and Carol's philosophy of sustainability.

Katy and Ollie had helped on other builds and Ollie is also a furniture maker and sculptor in wood, so they had the skills and experience necessary for the challenge. Ollie has been woodturning since he was seven years old and was inspired to use green wood by a local man, Stuart, who he met at a Weird and Wonderful Wood Festival.

Katy's works with communities with mental health issues, growing on a permaculture allotment and using willow for basket-making and sculpture. She is looking forward to having her own shed for willow work and already has a tin trough in front of the house for soaking the willow and making it pliable.

TOP John and Carol bought land that used to be a quarry and an orchard to build their strawbale house (see pages 184–87). They sold land to others who wanted to build sustainably, letting Katy and Ollie build a strawbale house on the last piece of land.

Some of the residents around them were resistant to the young couple, not only because they were building their own house, but because they were "not tidy." There were no valid planning objections, so, despite the delays, they could go ahead. They changed the planning permission to cover a smaller house to suit them and keep the trees. As they say, "It is like a little woodland with birds such as blackcaps and blue tits and fruit growing in the hedges." They explain that they want to "set a good example" of what is possible.

They moved into a caravan on the land four years ago and began to design and build their one-bedroom house. Ollie built a veranda on the caravan for food storage and for muddy boots and other paraphanalia. Katy says, "There is crap everywhere," but they have been lucky with a few mild winters, a wood-burning stove, and lots of free wood. The build began two and a half years ago and is still progressing.

ABOVE Ollie is a carpenter and woodsman with all the skills needed to build and create furniture, including a raised bed behind Katy's sculptural wall.

BELOW The house is still being built and Katy and Ollie are longing to move in. In the meantime, one of Ollie's beautifully made chairs sits on the pammented floor.

On the balustrade are some of Ollie's carvings and beautiful pieces of natural wood abound. They are using the shapes and grains of the wood in the build.

The bedroom contains a bed they made from beautiful wood—it sits high enough off the floor to provide some storage underneath. The floor in the bedroom is made from planed salvaged pallets, although it's hard to imagine that they come from such humble beginnings. The inner walls are made from wattle and daub, which is an ancient building method that uses split hazel and a mud mix, and they have left a bit showing as decoration and to ventilate the bathroom, which is unfinished at the moment.

Katy is filling the space between the living area and the bedroom with a sculptural wall of stones, fossils, and bottles that filter colored sunlight through the space. One of the windows is also lined with bottles, making it another decorative feature of the room.

The posts and bearers are made from spalted beech, with the fungus streaks creating a welcome pattern. They have two mature walnut trees that Ollie describes as "sentinels." All the units in the kitchen, as well as the organically shaped countertops, were made by Ollie. The NEFF oven

BOTTOM Ollie built the kitchen using his carpentry skills and using organic shapes for the countertops and local wood for the cabinets and shelves.

BELOW Katy has created a quirky window surround using glass and bottles.

ABOVE Ollie is a master of his craft and made this wooden chair with unusual spindles and turned wood.

came from a dumpster (skip) and the stovetops from ebay for £30 (US$ 40). The Rayburn cooker came from another online site and cost £100 (US$ 130).

This build has to happen around their work commitments, which means it is rather slow-going, but about 20 friends came to help clad the house in clay in return for food and an opportunity to enjoy the community spirit. As Katy and Ollie explain, "We sat outside and ate together... it was fun!"

The foundations are not deep, about a foot or so, as they hit hard chalk. They were able to use some chalk in the foundation plinth, but this is mostly built from flint stones gathered from surrounding land.

Straw bales were left over from John and Carol's build, as was a big roof timber that they were able to use. Boards came free from a local shipping company and sand from the quarry. The roof liner was an off-cut, which was big enough to cover the whole house. Pallets came from a local solar farm and clay from local farmers who were digging ditches.

The roof is made up in layers for strength and insulation. These layers include the pallets, pond liner, and two layers of carpets. They needed it to be strong enough to take the weight of a subsoil mix to support a living roof. They experimented with wild flowers for the bees, some of which actually live in a beehive on the roof. They say, "It looked beautiful a month ago." There are five other beehives on their land and John and Carol's land next door. They love bees and Katy is creating a bee pattern in the floor of the house. They also made sure the build included bird-nesting holes in the eaves. As they explain, "The birds moved in before we did."

Katy and Ollie will have a large porch on the north side for food storage, a composting toilet, and space for their work tools and boots. They comment, "We do mucky work."

The couple have more or less moved in permanently. They can't resist being there and are gradually moving from the caravan to the strawbale house.

BELOW Katy is in the process of making a mosaic in the floor, using hexagonal pamments to celebrate the honeycombs of the bees.

Carol and John are specialists in "slow building," having begun building their strawbale house eight years ago. They bought some land called "The Hollow," in Norfolk, England, and envisaged a plan for a "green" building. John says this is partially realized. They had planned to build a much larger home, but that was not to be. This building was only meant to be a studio, but it has morphed into their home. As they say, "It's tiny for us."

The strawbale house is set in timber framing. The interior is mainly comprised of one large space that incorporates a kitchen area, living space, and office and music space. They used a huge tripod and all their human resources to avoid having to bring in large machines. The huge timbers in the roof came from a sustainably managed wood on a nearby estate. John describes the scary process of using block and tackle, the Polish men who helped, and the strength and precision needed to position the beams exactly.

Carol and John did most of the building work themselves. John has carpentry skills and, with the help of an expert joiner who gave them confidence, they made all the interior fittings, as well as the main framework. It helped that the joiner's wife was an architect who could advise on structure and design. A friend was doing his MSc at the Centre for Alternative Technology, in Wales, and was anxious about the

ABOVE John and Carol are "slow builders" and are still finishing their strawbale house. They have laid a pathway around the outside walls to the rear of the welcoming organic house.

RIGHT The pathway leads to the north side of the building, which is perfect for a cool, shady porch for storing crops from the permaculture garden.

structure, insisting on "what we thought of as braces." They used a structural engineer to test for load-bearing and found it very stressful.

Carol had done a huge amount of research and the local council's building regulators passed the house, as there had been other strawbale home precedents. But, as Carol says, "They covered our butt!"

Around this curvaceous building, multi-colored quarry slates are used for the paths and continue onto the porch floor. The porch is also on the north side of the house, where they prepare and store produce and keep muddy boots out of the house.

Inside the floors are made from a limecrete mix with linseed and wax. The timing of the treatment of the floor with wax was affected by the time of year. It was important that the linseed sunk into the floor, but, because the temperature wasn't ideal, there is one area of the floor that isn't quite as hardy as the rest and this is protected with a rug. They joke, "Next year there will be a 're-finishing the floor' festival."

ABOVE The interior of the house is one large room, which serves as a kitchen, dining room, library, and music space, as well as a space for meditation and other social and learning activities. The tiny bedroom is off a balcony overlooking the room.

ABOVE The bathroom has a lovely, old-fashioned bathtub, which is freestanding. This room has soft red and green walls and a pamment floor.

BELOW John and Carol have two composting toilets, using one while the other is left to become compost. If it is left long enough, the compost is useful in the garden.

One of the most striking features of their living space is John's large cello that sits next to the stepladder! He is a musician in a band called "The John Preston Tribute Band," which plays gigs locally and beyond. In this space, they rehearse, show movies, and have discussions about permaculture design. The space acts as their library, too. All the books belong to Carol. She says that living in a rural area creates a cultural paucity and "I need books. I love learning and writing."

In the kitchen a musician friend, who is also a sculptor, created the beautiful floor mosaic of quarry slabs. On top of this, there's an island unit where many jars of pickled walnuts sit. Carol and John grow much of their own food in their gardens and get nuts and fruit from the trees around their house. They also have a bee-friendly garden, not only to encourage bees but also other pollinators for their crops, and to produce honey in beehives belonging to their neighbor, Kate.

Using permaculture design in all aspects of growing food and working with nature to maximize production is important to Carol and John. Even with good fencing, their efforts are sometimes impeded by pigeons, squirrels, and muntjac deer. The farthest zone from the house in an acre of land is the bank where ash trees do well.

They have two PulleyMaid™ racks suspended from the ceiling over the wood-burning Rayburn range to dry clothes indoors when the weather is too wet or the days too short.

As the strawbale house was first intended as a studio, there was originally no bedroom, so they created a small simple bedroom in the eaves that's accessed up some ladder stairs to a little balcony. In the bathroom a freestanding bathtub stands against walls painted with natural paints in green and soft red shades.

Other eco-friendly features in Carol and John's home include the recycling of water through a gray-water pond system, which filters the water through gravel and specially chosen plants to transform it into clean usable water. They also collect rainwater from their living roof, which they store in a large underground tank. Although they are not totally off-grid, they aim for closed systems of energy and water.

John says, "We are lagging behind on our solar grid because we picked up old-school collectors... and we forgot how to install them! We're not so good on the techno side... we prefer muck!" Indeed, John is an expert at composting. They have a two-chamber system with two toilets so that one can be closed down to produce compost while the other is in use.

They are not fans of the techno-fix solutions propounded to save our planet. The costs are too high and the ratios of the energy used to the energy produced keep on getting narrower. Carol says that new ways of building communities, sharing, and using less are a part of "re-imagining the future."

There is a green caravan in the garden, which serves as a writing and guest sleeping retreat. They have covered this with a traditional "shed" pantile roof on posts and, in future, there are thoughts of a building with a reciprocal timber roof for those music and mediation activities that all happen in their living room at present.

As Carol and John's explain, they are enjoying "de-coupling from the mainstream, having no mortgage, and the necessity to work is partially lifted. This enables us to do the work we love and offer what we have here to others... we are interested in connections which nourish us and cultural change."

ABOVE The kitchen is a busy space where meals are made and produce from the garden bottled for storing in an ample north-facing larder—the granite floors maintain a stable temperature.

ABOVE These ancient almshouses are no longer inhabited, but demonstrate a particular time in history when poor people could live behind the chapel.

Johnny is the Chair of the Trustees of this rare example of ancient almshouses in Glastonbury, in Somerset, England. Almshouses were a very early form of housing for poor people. The chapel and 16th-century almshouses stand on the grounds of the earlier Hospital of St. Mary Magdalene, which sheltered "ten poor men." There were once two rows of these little refuges, with a narrow flagstone alleyway between them. One row was knocked down in 1958, and this remaining row was restored at the same time. The almshouses were built with a "hodge podge" of stones, as they would originally have been whitewashed. These stones include Tor Burr, which is quarried next to Glastonbury Tor. Brick repairs would also have been hidden by the whitewash treatment.

In the Victorian era, the ten houses were converted to five houses and a washroom, since the first floors had to be removed because they had become too low, as people grew taller as the result of a better diet. Part of this original first floor has been recreated in the display almshouse. There would have been a spiral staircase or ladder to the upper floor. The floors are the original 16th-century flagstones, and some of the windows also date from that time. The height of the window lintel gives a clue to the original height of the floor and there is also an alcove in the fireplace that would have been a salt store.

This almshouse has been set up to look much as it would after the 19th-century renovations, including mostly Victorian furniture, imagining the occupant

BELOW The Trustees have furnished one of the almshouses in a simple and basic style, which it may have had after the 19th-century renovations.

as someone who had fought in the Boer War. The last occupants of the almshouses left in 1957.

There were individual allotments beyond the west wall. This land was then used for contemporary sheltered housing from the 1960s. Only an archway and a small paved area beyond remain.

The Hospital of St. Mary Magdalene dates back to at least the 13th century. There are records of "the gift and foundation of the Abbotts of Glastonbury" to house ten poor men before 1322. It was then an open-roofed hall with a central passageway and wooden cubicles on each side. As the original dedication was to Mary Magdalene, some of the first occupants may have been men suffering from leprosy, as Mary is the patron saint of lepers.

It is thought that the roof of the hospital was removed after England's Dissolution of the Monasteries in the 16th century, when Glastonbury Abbey and monastery were closed. Some of the building was demolished in the 1960s. The chapel and almshouses are Grade II listed and the foundations of the demolished almshouses are a scheduled ancient monument.

ABOVE Originally, there would have been stairs up to the sleeping balcony, where a Victorian bed suggests how the space would have been used. Below was somewhere to wash and eat.

The chapel is open daily for prayer, quiet, and contemplation. Today visitors can find their own place of rest and reflection in the beautiful hidden courtyard garden between the chapel and the almshouses.

INDEX

almshouses
Glastonbury 188–89
Suffolk 174–75
anti-materialism 7, 30
artwork 12, 29, 55, 71, 73, 75, 86, 88–89, 129, 172

Backcountry Tiny Homes 95
Baldry's Yard, Norfolk 26–29
bamboo flooring 35, 101, 117, 138
bathrooms and showers 18, 54, 60, 84, 99, 103, 106, 110, 111, 114–15, 142, 151, 186, 187
bedrooms and sleeping spaces 24, 25, 35, 42, 43, 48, 54, 55, 60, 66, 74, 77–78, 81, 85, 93, 97, 98, 99, 102–103, 105, 111, 115, 133, 135, 139, 141, 144, 169, 178–79, 182, 189
beekeeping 180, 183
Beetle Kill Pine 99
benders 162
Buddhist philosophy 149, 156

Caddy, Peter and Eileen 34, 126, 131
caravans 30, 160
Centires Terraces, Findhorn Foundation 134–35
co-housing movement 12
coaching inn conversion, Eye 176–79
communal facilities 8, 11, 12, 15, 18, 19, 34, 134
composting toilets 84, 144, 150, 186, 187
container houses 8, 11

contemporary spaces 10–35
Baldry's Yard, Norfolk 26–29
ecomobile home, Findhorn Foundation 30–35
micro-studios, Seattle 12–15
Tiny House Village, Seattle 16–21
workshop, converted, Cromer 22–25
Corian® 101
corrugated tin retro-retreat, Suffolk 70–75
cottages and houses 164–89
almshouse, Glastonbury 188–89
almshouse, Suffolk 174–75
coaching inn conversion, Eye 176–79
cottage by the bay, Forres 62–67
estate cottage, Suffolk 166–69
one-room-wide house, Bury St Edmunds 170–73
strawbale houses, Norfolk 180–87
Cranory 55
creativity 8–9
Crittall® windows 73

de-cluttering 7
debt-slavery culture 7, 97
dignity, human 15
Dutch barges
Maldon 37, 38–43
Norfolk 37, 44–49

Earthwool® 41

eco-homes 120–63
Honeypot, Findhorn Foundation 136–39
roundhouse, Somerset 156–59
row (terraced) house, Findhorn Foundation 134–35
shack, Norfolk 146–47
strawbale house, Glastonbury 152–55
treehouse, Norfolk 142–45
treehouse, Seattle 122–25
whisky barrel houses, Findhorn Foundation 126–33
yurt, Mongolian, Norfolk 148–51
yurt, Mongolian, Somerset 160–63
yurt (wooden roundhouse), Findhorn Foundation 140–41
ecomobile home, Findhorn Foundation 30–35
Edmunds, Nicole 126
energy efficiency 44
ergonomics 7
estate cottage, Suffolk 166–69
Everitt, Jon 71, 73
Eye of Heaven 150, 157, 158, 162

Findhorn Foundation, Forres 30–35, 62, 121, 126–45
fire safety 15, 24
floating homes 56
Lake Union, Seattle 52–55
flooring 35, 48, 66, 88, 101, 106, 112, 117, 138, 150, 154–55, 182, 185, 188

geo-energy 139
goat husbandry 82, 85

Haggard, Bill 52
Haggard, Riley 52
heat-exchange system 84
Heckler, Terry 55
Helmingham Hall 167
hemp lime 146
homelessness 8, 17, 18, 21, 26
Honeypot, Findhorn Foundation 136–39
horsebox lorry, Suffolk 82–85
Hospital of St Mary Magdalene 188–89
houseboats 8, 56
Lake Union, Seattle 56–61
housing market 7–8

insulation 41, 44, 64, 86, 91, 121, 129, 132, 153, 162
insurance 9, 101
International Building Code (IBC) 19

"Karma" building and co-housing, Seattle 12–15
kitchens and cooking facilities 14, 19, 24, 42, 52, 58, 73, 84, 97, 101, 106, 109, 110, 114, 128, 138, 149, 155, 157, 159, 179, 182–83, 186, 187

leaded windows 54
LED lighting 58, 84, 114
legality 6, 8
lime-washed paneling 42, 43
limecrete 185

living areas 25, 28, 29, 34, 35, 38, 41, 48, 52, 63, 66, 78, 88, 99, 101, 102, 106, 132, 135, 141, 144, 150, 154, 155, 168, 173, 175, 178, 185–86
Low Income Housing Institute (LIHI) 17, 18, 19, 21
low-money lifestyle 146
Lutheran Church of the Good Shepherd 17, 21

Maclean, Dorothy 34, 126, 131
Marmoleum 106
micro-studios, Seattle 12–15
minimalism 11, 24, 35, 41
Morris, William 7
multifunctional furniture 7
music systems 55, 58, 126

narrow boats *see* Dutch barges; floating homes; houseboats
National Organization of Alternative Housing (NOAH) 101
Nelson, Pete 122, 124
Neuman, David 14, 15
nomads 8

off-grid living 7, 121
roundhouse, Somerset 156–59
shack, Norfolk 146–47
yurt, Norfolk 148–51

permaculture 111, 159, 180, 186
pet animals 12, 21, 52, 56, 89, 99, 105, 106, 128
planning and zoning laws 8, 15
plants and gardens 23, 30, 74, 128, 135, 141, 145, 159, 166–67, 169, 171, 176, 178

Pocket Mansions 100–103
preacher's wagon, Norfolk 90–93
prefab units 11
public health issues 15

re-skilling 23, 151
Read, Sharon 109
reclaimed materials 24, 48, 66, 73, 88, 99, 119, 122, 150
Richards, Simon 134
roof terraces 12, 55
roofs
eco-friendly 35, 117, 139
link-way roofs 35, 139
living roofs 158, 183
roundhouses
Findhorn Foundation 140–41
Somerset 156–59

Sawhorse Revolution 19
Schumacher, E.F. 6, 103
Seattle Tiny Homes 108–11
shack, Norfolk 146–47
shakes (oak tiles) 153
showman's wagon, Suffolk 86–89
small efficiency dwelling units (SEDUs) 14
solar power 64, 84, 98, 111, 135, 146, 149, 150, 160
stairs
retractable 25
spiral staircases 61, 129
storage in 7, 41, 102, 109
star-gazing 35
stone flags 88, 154, 188
strawbale houses
Glastonbury 152–55
Norfolk 180–87
studio space 48, 89, 167, 171, 173, 174–75
see also artwork

Taizé 129

tiny homes
characteristics of 6
critical views of 14–15, 18
environmental benefits 7
legality 6, 8
off-grid 7, 121
part-time living 9, 69, 82
reasons for living in 6–7
Tiny House Village, Seattle 11, 16–21
Tiny Idahomes 112–15
treehouses
Norfolk 142–45
Seattle 122–25
Tumbleweed Tiny House 117

under-floor heating 121, 155

views 63, 66, 73, 85, 108, 111, 114, 125, 144, 145, 179
villages
Findhorn Foundation, Forres 30–35, 62, 121, 126–45
Tiny House Village, Seattle 11, 16–21
voluntary simplicity 30

wagon, Suffolk 76–81
Walker, Winifred 178
water, homes on or by 36–67
cottage by the bay, Forres 37, 62–67
Dutch barge, Maldon 37, 38–43
Dutch barge, Norfolk 37, 44–49
floating home, Lake Union, Seattle 37, 52–55
houseboat, Lake Union, Seattle 37, 56–61
water-collection and recycling systems 150, 187

wattle and daub 155, 182
wheels, tiny homes on 68–119
corrugated tin retro-retreat, Suffolk 70–75
custom-designed, King County 104–107
custom-designed, Seattle 94–103
custom-designed, Washington State 108–19
horsebox lorry, Suffolk 82–85
preacher's wagon, Norfolk 90–93
showman's wagon, Suffolk 86–89
wagon, Suffolk 76–81
whisky barrel houses, Findhorn Foundation 126–33
wildlife watching 77, 85, 95, 111, 115, 151
wind power 139
Wishbone Tiny Homes 118
wood-burning stoves 34, 48, 66, 78, 84, 91, 92, 115, 121, 129, 132, 141, 150, 153, 157, 158, 166
workshops, converted
Baldry's Yard, Norfolk 26–29
Cromer 22–25
World Wide Opportunities on Organic Farms (WWOOF) 156, 160

yurts
Mongolian yurt, Norfolk 148–51
Mongolian yurt, Somerset 160–63
wooden roundhouse, Findhorn Foundation 140–41

ACKNOWLEDGMENTS

I would like to thank all those who have taken part in the creation of this book and all those who have helped me find the varied and fascinating examples of people living in tiny homes. I would especially like to thank Nicolette Hallett for her patience, driving, and understanding of how I work, and also her great photos. Last, but not least, I thank family and friends for their support.

Thanks to all the tiny homes builders, owners, and enablers who allowed us to photograph their places and tell their stories: Emma and Andrew Aldous (creators of Queenie); Lee Atkinson (boat designed and renovated by owner Lee Atkinson, taking five years from purchase date); Kevin and Linda Bagley; Carly Balster and Jennifer Balangue; Wendy Black; Loraine Burr; Christine Burton; Linda Chawner and Antje Ernestus (new build in Cromer, Norfolk); Carmen Corinne (Carmen Corinne's house in Washington state, designed by Carmen Corinne. Jesse Collingsworth, builder, owner of Tiny Idahomes.); Mari Cormier; Hannah Rose Crabtree (Hannah's home in West Seattle, built and designed by Hannah Rose Crabtree of

Pocket Mansions.); Sally Cvetovac (Sally Cvetovac's home in Seattle, designed by Bill Haggard (Haggard Houseboats) and Alex Wilken (Seattle Boat Works); Roger Doudna (Roger Doudna's home in the Findhorn Community, Scotland. Keith Wilcox, Australian architect and one-time Findhorn gardener); Katy Fullilove and Oliver Brunton (Katy and Oliver's home in Norfolk, designed with and enabled by Carol Hunter and John Preston. They would like to thank all the friends and family who have given their time, energy and enthusiasm over the course of the build); Sally Goldsmith (Sally's home built by Jon Everett); Alexis Haifley (Alexis and Brian's home in Washington state designed and built in collaboration with Backcountry Tiny Homes; Julie Ham (interiors and artwork by Julie Ham); Chris and Tatiana Hankins; Devin Hanley (also Paul and Diane Hanley, and Jack Dalton); Johnny Heriz-Smith, Royal Magdalene Almshouses, Glastonbury, restored by Heriz Payne Architects, Glastonbury; Carol Hunter and John Preston (house designed and built by Carol Hunter and John Preston, with the generous help of friends and family; also Cary Outis, Les Chappell, Terry Glen, Fred Heath Preston, Mark Saich from 3HAI); Ryan and Daphne Jacobsen; Johann and Firefly; John and Mary L; Alan and Muriel Lacey (Alan and Muriel's home in the Broads, designed and fitted out by them during the 1990s, when moored in Malden, Essex); Dürton Lau (Dürton Lau's home, owned by The Findhorn Foundation and designed and built by Rolf Iverson); LIHI and the residents of the Seattle Tiny House Village; Gosia Malgorzata; Graham Meltzer; Dee Nickerson and Richard Hunter; George P; Andy Portman (Andy Portman's home in Somerset, designed and built by Andy and Ella Portman, with community support. Ella Portman: designer. Paul Horton: timber-frame designer. Robert Greenfield led the making of the timber frame with Andy); Sibylle Rhovier; Bryony and Liam Richardson (Bryony and Liam's home, design by ECO Village Ltd, architect Simon Richards, engineer John Talbot); Jo Rodriquez; Annette and Mike Rolston; Auriol de Schmidt; Bill Seaman and Janine Oxley (Bill and Janine's preacher's wagon, renovated by Bill); Mark and Kara Stacey (Mark and Kara's home in Washington state built by Seattle Tiny Homes; Marcus Tribe (Marcus's home, Nomansland, Devon, made by Marcus Tribe. Kitchen designed and fitted by Ben Ranson of Barrel Top Wagons); John Willoner and Sylvie Black (John Willoner's home, architect Stephen Fretton).